Ancient Epistle of Barnabas

His Life and Teaching

by
Ken Johnson, Th.D.

Ancient Epistle of Barnabas
by Ken Johnson, Th.D.

Printed in the United States of America

ISBN 1450583822
EAN-13 9781450583824

Unless otherwise indicated, Bible quotations are the actual quotes from the ancient church fathers and not from any modern Bible version.

Table of Contents

Introduction to the Epistle of Barnabas

Who Was Barnabas?
Barnabas was born in Salamis, Cyprus. Both of his parents were Jewish, descended from the tribe of Levi (Acts 4:36).

According to the *Recognitions of Clement* 1.7.1-1.11.8, Barnabas was the first Christian to witness in Rome. Clement of Rome heard him preach and later converted to Christianity.

Barnabas is listed as one of the New Testament prophets who resided at Antioch (Acts 13:1). Luke described him as "a good man, full of the Holy Spirit and of faith" and remarked that he brought a considerable number of people to the Lord (Acts 11:24).

Barnabas introduced the newly converted Paul to the apostles and attested to the fact that Paul was now truly a Christian (Acts 9:27). He traveled on mission trips with the Apostle Paul (Acts 14:8-12).

Ancient church father Theodorus Lector, in his work, *Ecclesiastical History* 2.557, stated that Barnabas and Paul studied together in the school of Gamaliel. Barnabas had often tried to witness to Paul, but he would have none of it until his conversion on the road to Damascus.

Galatians 2 records that when Peter fell into error regarding Jewish food laws, he persuaded Barnabas to follow along in the error. Only Paul was able to see this error and the reasons why this was wrong are recorded in the book of Hebrews. This may explain why the Epistle of Barnabas is very similar to Hebrews.

Ancient church fathers Hippolytus, in his work *The Seventy*, Clement of Alexandria, in *Stromata 2*, and Eusebius, in *Ecclesiastical History 1.12*, all teach Barnabas was one of the seventy disciples that Jesus sent out (Luke 10:1,17). If this is true, Barnabas would have been an eyewitness of our Lord.

When Barnabas died, he was buried in his native country of Cyprus.

What Is The Epistle Of Barnabas?
The Epistle of Barnabas is an epistle written for the purpose of teaching Christians about typological prophecy. This epistle was highly valued and quoted by the ancient church fathers.

When Was The Epistle Of Barnabas Written?
There are no dates assigned to it from ancient sources. It was written after the destruction of the Temple in AD 70, because the Temple's destruction is cited in chapter 16.

What Ancient Manuscripts Still Exist?
The Epistle of Barnabas is included in the Codex Sinaiticus, a Greek uncial Bible dating from the fourth century AD. A facsimile edition of the Sinaiticus can be obtained from Clarendon Press.

The Codex Hierosolymitanus, a Greek Bible dating about AD 1056, contains the Epistle of Barnabas.

A Latin manuscript of the Epistle of Barnabas exists in St. Petersburg, dating from the end of the fourth century (St Petersburg, Q.v.I.39).

Who Is The Author Of The Epistle Of Barnabas?

According to the ancient church fathers, it was written by the same Barnabas who was the apostle Paul's companion, one of the seventy disciples Jesus sent out two by two. This is probably why the Epistle of Barnabas is included in the Codex Sinaiticus as Scripture.

The Epistle was held in very high esteem by the ancient church. Clement of Alexandria referred to it as Scripture and believed it was written by Barnabas, Paul's companion (*Stromata* 2.6-7, 17). Origen referred to it as a general epistle (*Against Celsus* 1.63), and listed it among the Scriptures (*Commentary on Romans* 1.24). Jerome regarded it as genuine and held it in very high esteem. Eusebius, however, regarded it as spurious (*Ecclesiastical History* 3.25.4).

Almost all scholars of the eighteenth and nineteenth centuries accepted the Epistle as a genuine epistle written by Barnabas. Modern liberal scholarship concludes it could not be from the first century, based on numerous errors and a firm anti-Semitic tone. However, they accept Paul's writings in the New Testament to be genuine and yet seemingly anti-Semitic. They also fail to recognize that the Epistle of Barnabas has not been preserved perfectly as part of the canon and has been corrupted in several places by scribal errors. This is one reason why it should not be included in the canon.

Martin Luther made the same mistake when he used a corrupted Latin version of the Epistle of James, and then concluded it should be removed from the canon of Scripture.

Modern "scholars" also teach that since the book of Daniel is so accurate with its prophecies up to the first coming of the Messiah, it can't possibly be genuinely written by Daniel in the fifth century BC. They teach someone in the first century AD. basically lied, calling himself Daniel and writing history as if it was future prophecy.

Real Christians believe in Bible prophecy and instead take these facts as a sign that the book of Daniel is indeed real. We should look at the Epistle of Barnabas in the same way, but should not call it Scripture.

Why Was The Epistle of Barnabas Written?
The Epistle of Barnabas was written to teach Christians about typological prophecy. It is very similar to the Biblical book of Hebrews; and some have speculated that Hebrews was also written by Barnabas. In his *Ecclesiastical History*, Eusebius said the Apostle Paul wrote Hebrews to a group of Jews in the Hebrew language and Luke translated it into Greek. This would explain why some parts sound like Paul and others do not.

Since the ancient church fathers taught Paul wrote Hebrews it was included in the canon. Some of the ancient church fathers said this epistle was written by "a" Barnabas. The simple fact that we are not sure if the author was truly the same Barnabas who accompanied Paul and was an eye witness of our Lord give us another reason why it should not be added to the Canon of Scripture. However, like many other ancient church documents, it should be studied to give insight into the teachings of the first two centuries AD.

This Translation
I have endeavored to translate this Epistle into modern English based on the idea that the writer would have been a conservative first century Christian who knew well the

Epistle of Barnabas

Gospel and the prophecies. Where Scripture is quoted, I have left the quote as is in the Epistle and just referenced what the author was quoting.

Problems
Some of the problems with previous translations occur because the Epistle is written in Greek; but Barnabas spoke Hebrew. Hebrew idioms directly translated into Greek and then directly translated into English are usually very confusing. Also, in various places the Greek and Latin versions were highly corrupted.

Some believe the writer of the epistle was anti-Semitic, but instead, he was simply pointing out many of the typological prophecies widely believed by Bible-believing Christians today. Here are some arguments against, and answers for, the Epistle of Barnabas.

1. The Epistle was written after the destruction of the Jerusalem Temple in AD 70, but the apostolic Barnabas supposedly died about AD 64.

   This means either the date for Barnabas' death is wrong or this epistle was written by another Barnabas. This uncertainty about the author is one reason it was not added to the canon of Scripture.

   The epistle mentions baptism but not the Eucharist; and the importance of meeting in church, but does not mention any kind of higher clergy. It also mentions the gift of prophecy. These facts suggest it was written before the late second century when the doctrines about these subjects began to change.

2. The whole tone of the book seems anti-Semitic. Since Barnabas was a Jew from the tribe of Levi, it is unlikely that he wrote the epistle.

   Paul was so strong in his Jewish faith that he persecuted the Christian church, but upon his conversion he wrote Galatians and Hebrews – between AD 50 and 67 – both of which seem more anti-Semitic than this epistle.

3. Barnabas interprets circumcision and the Jewish food laws as purely spiritual.

   Barnabas points out that circumcision and the Jewish food laws are like the rituals performed during the festivals; they are real, but also show typological prophecies. Barnabas never meant to say these things did not take place or were made up stories. See the following section on typological prophecies.

4. Barnabas makes additions to Jewish rituals that are not recorded anywhere else, leaving us to conclude he invented the additions.

   This is not completely true. Some additions, like the cliffs where the Yom Kippur goat was killed, are recorded in the Mishna. The details that are not recorded anywhere else may have been the way the Jews performed the ritual in his day, whether or not they were supposed to.

5. Barnabas seems to use Bible codes in chapter 9 to show Abraham's 318 men were a typological prophecy pointing to Christ.

Epistle of Barnabas

> Since the ancient church fathers did not use "Bible codes" and spoke of them as "a waste of time and a distraction from Satan," I conclude this part was an addition to the original text.

6. This epistle mentions the destruction of the Temple in Jerusalem and the prophecy of Daniel's four beasts. Connecting these two seems to indicate Barnabas was an amillennialist. Since all ancient church fathers were premillennialists, this would indicate it was written by an Alexandrian Christian after the amillennialist position began to take hold in Egypt, about AD 190.

> Nowhere does the epistle indicate an amillennialist position. Chapter 4 clearly teaches a future tribulation period. Chapter 16 teaches the Jews would be dispersed, then return and rebuild their Temple. Chapter 15 teaches that the Thousand-year Reign of Christ will occur at the end of six thousand years of human history, which is when the Antichrist is destroyed at the Second Coming of Christ. Chapter 6 teaches we are not in the Millennium yet because we have no dominion over the animals, nor do we have our glorified bodies. Therefore, the author must have been a premillennialist, which indicates it very well could have been written in the first century.

Typological Prophecies
In addition to literal prophecies where a prophet will simply tell of a future event, there are typological prophecies where a ritual taught about a future event.

There is a big difference between an allegory and a type! An allegory is a fictitious story made up to point out a

10

moral truth; whereas a typological prophecy is a real, literal, ritual which points to a future event.

The ritual of the Passover lamb was a literal ritual that has been practiced for over 3,000 years, but points to Jesus' death on the cross. The Passover lamb was typological like many of the types pointed out by Paul and the book of Hebrews.

Philo and Origin took the concept of typological prophecies too far and were well known for their allegories. These men would say every passage of Scripture has some hidden spiritual meaning, which, of course, is not true. We need to be careful not to add to the Scriptures.

There are many Jewish laws and ceremonies that contain typological prophecies pointing to the Messiah.

Basic Points of the Text
The basic teachings in the Epistle of Barnabas are that the animal sacrifices, Yom Kippur Fast, circumcision, Jewish food laws, and the Sabbath, have been abolished because they simply pointed to Christ. The Epistle goes on to point out many other things that are typological. The chart on the following page shows where Barnabas and other passages in the New Testament teach the true meanings of other typological prophecies

Underlying Theme
The underlying theme of the Epistle of Barnabas is the concept of a three-fold witness. The idea is given that every mature Christian should be able to teach the plan of salvation, creation history and creation science, and prophecy to anyone who will listen. Prophecy is both

Epistle of Barnabas

literal and typological and we should focus on the prophecies fulfilled during our lifetime.

Prophecy proves inspiration	Barn. 1; 2 Pet. 1:19-21
Animal sacrifices abolished	Barn. 2; Heb. 10:1-14
Revived Roman Empire	Barn. 4; Dan. 7; 2 Thess. 2
Yom Kippur	Barn. 7; Heb. 9
Red heifer, a type of Christ	Barn. 8; Heb. 9
Circumcision abolished	Barn. 9; Acts 15, Titus 1
Food laws abolished	Barn. 10; Gal. 2
Baptism prefigured in the OT	Barn. 11; 1 Pet. 3
The cross prefigured in the OT	Barn. 12
Christian heirs to the covenant	Barn. 13
New covenant	Barn. 14; Heb. 8
Sabbath abolished	Barn. 15; Heb. 4
Temple temporarily destroyed	Barn. 16; Heb. 8

Moses Breaking the Ten Commandments

A Typological Prophecy of the Coming New Covenant

1
Eternal Life, Creation, and Prophecy

[1]Greetings, sons and daughters, in the name of our Lord Jesus Christ, who loved us in peace. [2]I exceedingly rejoice in your blessed and admirable spirit, seeing that you abound in the knowledge of the oracles of God, because you have fully received the spiritual gifts and have been grafted into the olive tree.[a] [3]This is why I am overjoyed in the hope of salvation. I longed for, and am now amazed, to truly see the Holy Spirit poured out among you so richly with the Lord's love. [4]I am even more fully convinced of this because, since I spoke of these things to you, I have learned much in the way of righteousness. I also truly love you beyond my own soul, because of your love and great faith in the hope of eternal life. [5]For this reason I took the time to write to you some of the things I have learned. It will do me good to minster to you and I was eager to send you this small letter to make your faith and knowledge more perfect.

The Three-Fold Witness

[6]There are three points of our faith that the Lord has ordained that we have full knowledge of: the hope of eternal life, the world's true history, and prophecy. [7]For the Lord has declared to us by His prophets the things that happened long ago, the prophecies we see being fulfilled in our lifetime, and has also given us the first-fruits of the knowledge of future events. [8]So, when we see these prophecies fulfilled, one by one, we should be more reverent when approaching His altar[b]. [9]I wish to

---

[a] Grafted in olive tree; see Romans 11
[b] This is a reference to communion, see 1 Corinthians 11:23-24.

reveal a few things to you, not as your teacher, but as a fellow Christian. I know you will be very excited about these truths, considering your present circumstances!

Commentary

Barnabas wrote this epistle to his students. They were following all the commands laid down in the New Testament and were experiencing the gifts of the Holy Spirit; but to be mature in their faith; they were told to spend their time focusing on what Barnabas calls the Three-Fold Witness. In other words, this means that a mature Christian must understand, and be able to explain to others, three main points of the Christian faith.

First, they are to know how to explain everything related to Salvation. This would mean being able to tell others about the Creation and Fall of Man, the sin nature, and the need for salvation; how Jesus, second person of the Trinity, incarnated in human form to live a sinless life and die on the cross to pay for all of our sins, and that the gift of eternal life is free to all those who repent.

Second, the fact of creation is very important. Many of the ancient church fathers taught that in the last days, when the great apostasy would invade the church, the teaching of evolution would replace the teaching of creation.

Third, they were to understand all the prophecies and be able to show others that the events that have happened in their lifetime are fulfillments of ancient prophecies.

To be mature Christians, we should do the same. Each one of us should be able to answer any question regarding sin and salvation, creation, and prophecy. To this end I have created the books _Ancient Post-Flood History,_ and _Ancient Prophecies Revealed,_ giving a detailed look at the secular historical documents that prove Creationism and the Flood, and to show that in modern times over 53 biblical prophecies have been fulfilled between AD 1948 and 2008. See the last three chapters of this book for more details.

2
Animal Sacrifices Abolished

¹Seeing that the days are evil, and that Satan is in control of this world, we ought to give all the more diligence to perfect our knowledge of the Three-Fold Witness. ²Reverance, patience, longsuffering, and self-restraint will aid us in our faith. ³While these things keep us pure in regard to the Lord, we must add to them wisdom, understanding, science, and knowledge. ⁴For God has revealed to us by all the prophets that He no longer wants sacrifices, burnt offerings, or oblations. He said,

> "'What are the multitude of your sacrifices to Me?' says the LORD. 'I have had enough of burnt offerings of rams and the fat of fed cattle. I don't take any pleasure in the blood of bulls, lambs or goats when you come to appear before Me. Who required you to trample My courts? Don't bring your worthless offerings to Me any longer. Your incense is an abomination to Me and I can't put up with your New Moons and Sabbaths. Even your solemn assembly is iniquity. I hate your New Moon Festivals and your appointed feasts.'"
>
> *Based on Isaiah 1:11-14*

⁶Therefore, God has abolished these things that the new law of our Lord Jesus Christ, free from the yoke of such necessity, might have an offering not made by human hands. ⁷Again God said;

> "Did I command your fathers when they came out of the land of Egypt to offer me burnt offerings and sacrifices? No! This is what I commanded them…

let none of you devise evil in your heart against his neighbor, and do not love perjury."
Based on Jeremiah 7:22-23; Zecharaih 8:17

[9]So we ought to know, unless we are void of common sense, the gracious intention of our heavenly Father. [10]For He speaks to us desiring that we should not go astray like them, but to understand how we can approach Him. [11]God had declared;

"The only sacrifice pleasing to God is a broken spirit; a broken and contrite heart God will not despise." *Based on Psalm 51:17*

[13]Therefore brethren, we ought to accurately learn about those things that belong to our salvation, so the wicked one will not deceive us into losing our spiritual life.

Commentary
Hebrews 10:12,14,18 teach that Jesus was the one and only sacrifice. We now have sacrifices of praise (Hebrews 13:15). The animal sacrifices simply pointed to the ultimate sacrifice Jesus made for us when He died on the cross. The rituals of animal sacrifices were typological prophecies that pointed to Jesus' death and our atonement.

3

Yom Kippur Fast Abolished

Again God says;

> "Why do you fast to Me like you do today to make your voice heard on high? You humble yourself, bow your head, put on sackcloth and ashes, and call it an acceptable fast, but it is not. The fast I have chosen is to loosen every bond of wickedness, break harsh agreements, restore to liberty those who are bruised, and tear in pieces every unjust bond. Feed the hungry with your bread, clothe the naked, bring the homeless poor into your house, don't despise the humble, and don't turn away members of your own family. Then your light will break out like the dawn, your healing will come quickly, righteousness will go before you, and the glory of God will surround you. Then you will call, and the LORD will answer and while you are still speaking He will say 'Here I am,' if you free others, don't swear falsely, or murmur, give your food to the poor with a cheerful heart, and show compassion on the afflicted." *Based on Isaiah 58:4-10*

[20]Brethren, in this passage God has proven by His foreknowledge and love for us, that the people whom He has purchased for His beloved Son were to believe in sincerity; therefore, showing all these things to us, we should not run as proselytes to Jewish law.

Chapter 3

Commentary

In this chapter Barnabas explains that passages like Isaiah 58:4-10 not only showed God hated it when the priests would just go through the motions of fasting on the Day of Atonement (also called Yom Kippur), instead of truly repenting. The fast commanded on the Day of Atonement was supposed to teach us to abstain from wickedness and give to those who are in need.

Zechariah 7:4-10 also taught that a true fast is giving your food to those who really need it. The rabbis had no right to declare new days of fasting. God ordained only one: Yom Kippur, the Day of Atonement.

Some thought fasting would automatically guarantee an answer to prayer (Isaiah 58:3-4). Against this, the prophets taught that without proper understanding and conduct, fasting was useless (Isaiah 58:5-12; Jeremiah 14:11-12; Zechariah 7).

These passages indicate that, since the fast is a typological prophecy that pointed to our need to repent and accept Jesus' death on the cross, we need no longer observe the Yom Kippur Fast, nor any other fast created by the ancient rabbis.

4

The Prophecy of the Ten Kingdoms

End Time Prophecy

[1]We ought to earnestly inquire into the events prophesied to occur in our present age, and search the Scriptures for those things which pertain to salvation. [2]We must completely flee the works of iniquity lest they overcome us. [3]And let us hate this present satanic deception, and set our love on the world to come. [4]Let us give no freedom to our souls to have power to run with sinners and wicked men, lest we be made like them.

The final days of the Tribulation will come as prophesied by the Scripture,

> "For this reason, the Lord will cut short[c] the times and the days, that His beloved might quickly come into His inheritance."
> *Based on Matthew 24:22 and Malachi 3:1*

[7]And the prophet Daniel also prophesied,

> "Ten kings will reign from the heart of the earth, and a little king will rise up after them, who will subdue three of the kings and create one united kingdom." *Based on Daniel 7:24*

[8]Daniel again spoke about the same kingdoms saying,

> "I beheld a fourth beast, wicked and powerful, extremely strong, and more savage than all the

---

[c] See Matthew 24:15-23

beasts of the earth. From it sprang up ten horns, and then a little one appeared, and it subdued three great horns and formed one kingdom."
Based on Daniel 7:7-8

Only Christians Have Eternal Life

[10]You ought to be able to understand this also. I ask one thing of you, as one who loves you more than my own soul; watch out that you don't pile sin upon sin like those who say that our covenant [of eternal life] pertains to both [non-messianic] Jews and Christians. [11]It is ours alone!

Moses' Prophecy of a New Covenant

They have permanently lost that which Moses received. [12]For the Scripture says,

"Moses fasted forty days and nights on the mount, and received the covenant of the Lord, along with the Ten Commandments, written with the finger of God." *Based on Exodus 31:18; 34:28*

[14]But they lost it when they turned to idols. The Lord said to Moses,

"Come down quickly, for your people, whom you brought out of the land of Egypt, have corrupted themselves." *Based on Exodus 32:7 and Deuteronomy 9:12*

[16]Moses understood [this prophetic meaning], and threw the two stone tablets from his hands. Their covenant was broken into pieces, prophetically symbolizing that the new covenant of the love of Jesus might be placed in our hearts,[d] in the hope which flows from believing in Him.

---

[d] See Jeremiah 31:31-34

Godliness

[17]Let us pay close attention to godliness as we see the end times approaching. For our whole life of faith will mean nothing if unless we now, as becomes the sons of God, remain pure. [18]Satan will not deceive us into temptation if we totally hate wickedness. So let us flee all vanity, entirely hating all evil. [19]Don't live a solitary life, forgetting to assemble together, like you were already made perfect[e]. Come together in one place to make common inquiry of the Scriptures. For the Scripture says,

"Woe to them that are wise in their own eyes, and prudent in their own sight." *Based on Isaiah 5:21*

[21]Let us be spiritually minded, one holy Temple[f], dedicated to God. As much as it lies within us, let us fear God, keep His commandments, and rejoice in the prophecies! [22]The Lord will judge the world without respect to persons. Each will receive as he has done[g]: if he is righteous, his righteousness will precede him; if he is wicked, the reward of wickedness is before him. [23]Never rest as though we were 'called' and slumber in our sins, lest Satan gain power over us and thrust us out from the Kingdom of the Lord[h]. [24]Brothers, please understand this also; so many signs and wonders happened in Israel, yet they were ignored; so pay close attention to the prophecies, lest we be found as the Scripture says,

"Many are called but few are chosen."
Based on Matthew 22:14

---

[e] See Hebrews 10:25
[f] See 1 Corinthains 3:16
[g] Bema Judgment Seat and Revelation 20:12, 13
[h] See Parable of the Ten Virgins

Commentary

The main point of this chapter is that the prophecies of Daniel's four beasts were partially fulfilled when Rome (the fourth beast) destroyed the Temple as predicted in Micah and Daniel. Since the prophecies will be completely fulfilled with the destruction of the Antichrist at the end of the Tribulation, Christians should be very aware of the prophecies and await the Rapture while remaining pure in morals and doctrine.

Many of the ancient church fathers thought that Moses' breaking the ten commandments and carving a new set was a type of the New Covenant we have in Christ.

The Aposlte Paul showed that there were many such typological prophecies. Here are some of them.

Typological prophecies from the book of Hebrews

Vs		
Heb 4:9	Weekly Sabbath	Millennial reign (no Mosaic works)
Heb 9:2	Outer tabernacle/Holy place	The Church
Heb 9:2	Lampstand	The light of the world
Heb 9:2	Table of Showbread (faces)	Christ's incarnation
Heb 9:3	Holy of Holies	Throne room of God / Heaven
Heb 9:3	Second veil split in two	All go boldly before the throne of God
Heb 9:4	Altar of incense	Prayers of the saints (Rev. 8:4)
Heb 9:4	Ark of the Covenant	Christ
Heb 9:4	Golden jar of manna	Bread of life, hidden manna (Rev. 2:17)
Heb 9:4	Aaron's rod	(Num. 17:1-8)
Heb 9:4	Tablets of the Covenant	(Deut. 10:1-5)
Heb 9:5	Cherubim	Four living creatures
Heb 9:5	Mercy seat – covering	Atonement
Heb 9:7	Yom Kippur ritual	Christ
Heb 9:13	Ashes of the red heifer	Christ
Heb 9:19	Scarlet wool & hyssop	Made clean by the blood of the Lamb
Heb 10:22	Water basin	Pure conscience
Heb 13:2	Red heifer burned outside the camp	Jesus crucified outside Jerusalem's walls

Epistle of Barnabas

Typological prophecies from the New Testament

Mt 12:40	Sign of Jonah	Jesus buried for three days
Jn 3:14	Brazen serpent	Jesus lifted up on the cross
Rom 4	Abraham father of uncircumcised	The two covenants
Rom 5	Second Adam	Christ
1Cor 10:3,4	Rock that flowed with water	Represented Christ
1Cor 10:3,4	Manna, cloud & sea- baptism	Salvation
2Cor 3:7	Moses' glory faded	The old covenant would fade
2Cor 3:14	Veil over Moses' face	Not leaving Moses for Christ
Gal 4:22	Sarah/Hagar	Old and new covenants
Gal 4:21-31	Sinai engenders bondage	Legalism
Gal 4:21-31	New Jerusalem	Gives freedom
Gal 4:21-31	Isaac	Gen 22:8,18 child of promise
Gal 4:21-31	Ishmael	Gen 22:8,18 child of promise
Eph 2:14	Middle wall of partition broken	Jew & Gentile are one body
Col 2:11	Circumcision	A pure heart
Col 2:17	Food, drink, new moon, Sabbath, seven festivals	Point to Christ
1 Pet 2:4-9	Chief cornerstone	Christ
1 Pet 3:20-22	Noah's Flood	A type of baptism

Typological prophecies from the Old Testament

Num 2	Israeli camp forms a cross	Salvation though the cross
Ex 17:9-12	Moses has to form a cross for Israelis to win a battle	Salvation though the cross
Num 20:8	Moses strikes rock, instead of speaking to it	By his power, not reliance on Holy Spirit – Gal 3:1-3
	Moses broke 10 Commandments	New covenant coming
	Moses carved second set	Jesus replaces old covenant
Isaiah 53	Matzah stripes (Passover)	Jesus' stripes
Num 35:28	Murders forgiven when current high priest dies	Jesus is our forgiveness
Lev 10:1-2	Nadab & Abihu – strange fire	Salvation only though Jesus
2King 6:5	Axe floating - Elijah	Salvation though the cross
Ex 15:23	Wood to fix bitter water	Salvation through the cross
	Nebuchadnezzar's Image & 666	Antichrist
Dan. 3	Shadrach, Meshach, and Abednego	Jews in the Tribulation
Dan. 3	Daniel	Raptured church
Gen 25:23	Rebecca's two children	The two covenants
Gen 48:9-11	Joseph's two children	The two covenants

Yom Kippur is a typological prophecy

of the Second Coming

5

The Crucifixion Prophesied

[1]The reason our Lord gave up His body to destruction was to cleanse us through the remission of sins by the sprinkling of His blood. [2]The Scripture contains some things about Him partly relating to Israel and partly to us. It says,

> "He was wounded for our transgressions, bruised for our iniquities, and by His stripes we are healed... He was brought as a sheep to the slaughter, and as a lamb which is dumb before its shearer." *Based on Isaiah 53:5, 7*

[4]Therefore we ought to be deeply grateful to the Lord; for He has revealed the true history of the earth, given us wisdom for the present, and left us with the predictions of the future. [5]Now the Scripture says,

> "Not unjustly is the net spread for the birds."
> *Based on Proverbs 1:17*

[6]This means that a man who knows the way of righteousness, but turns aside into the way of darkness, deserves to perish. [7]Remember it was to Jesus, God said,

> "Let us make man in our own image,"
> *Based on Genesis 1:26*

[9]Make sure you can explain to others why our Lord, who made us in His image, suffered for our souls. [10]The ancient prophets, who received their spiritual gift from Him, prophesied that the Messiah was to abolish death

and reveal the resurrection from the dead. [11]He incarnated and died to fulfill the promise to the fathers, and to prepare a new people for Himself. The fact of His resurection proves He will also come back to judge the world.

His Incarnation
[12]Another thing, during His first coming, He loved the people of Israel greatly and preached the good news to them, teaching them with great signs and wonders. [13]When He chose His twelve apostles to preach His Gospel, they were sinners above all, showing He came

"not to call the righteous, but sinners to repentance."
Based on Matthew 9:13

[14]Then He manifested Himself to be the true Son of God. [15]For if He had not come in the flesh, how could men have been saved by beholding Him? [16]Just as men can't stare at the sun, which will cease to exist, but was created by Jesus, they could not behold Him until He was made flesh. [17]He came in the flesh to judge those who persecuted and slew His prophets.

Prophecies of the Crucifixion
[18]This is also a reason for His death. [19]For about the flogging of Jesus, God said,

"The wounds of His flesh are from them... When they shall smite their own shepherd, then the sheep of the flock shall be scattered."
Based on Zechariah 13:7

[21]It was God's plan all along that Jesus should suffer on the cross. The prophecies said,

> "Spare My soul from the sword..."
> *Based on Psalm 22:20*

[23] And,

> "They pierce My flesh with nails, for the synagogue of the wicked has risen up against Me... They pierced My hands and My feet."
> *Based on Psalm 22:16*

[24] And again He says,

> "Behold, I have given My back to scourging, My cheeks to be smitten, and I have set My face as a firm rock." *Based on Isaiah 50:6*

Commentary

This chapter teaches that it was God's plan all along that Jesus would incarnate and die for the sins of the people. Jesus created everything with God the Father. The world was created; it never evolved. These truths were taught in many places in the Old Testament, both literally and typologically.

The Scripture reveals the true history of the earth; Creation and the Flood. The ancient church fathers taught that in the last days the church would apostsize and replace the biblical teaching of Creation with the pagan concept of evolution. Mature Christians know how to share their faith, not just about eternal life and how they got saved, but about current fulfilled prophecy. And they know how to combat evolution. See the last three chapters for a detailed discussion on how to do this.

6

New Creation Prophecied

¹When He had fulfilled the commandment, what did He say?

> "Who will contend with Me? Let him oppose Me. Who has a case against Me? Let him draw near to Me. Woe to you! Because you will all become old as a garment, the moth will eat you up."
> *Based on Isaiah 50:8-9*

The Cornerstone

³Again the Prophet said He was placed as a strong stone for crushing,

> "Behold, I lay in Zion for a foundation, a precious stone, a precious and honorable cornerstone."
> *Based on Isaiah 8:14, 28:16 NASB*

⁴What did the Prophet say next?

> "He who believes in Him will live forever."
> *Based on Isaiah 28:16 LXX, 1 Peter 2:6*

⁵Is our hope set on a stone? Absolutely not! The prophet is referring to our Lord's flesh being His strength. For He said,

> "He placed Me as a firm rock." *Based on Isaiah 50:7*

⁷And He also said,

"The stone which the builders rejected has become the chief cornerstone... This is the great and wonderful day, which the Lord made..."
Based on Psalm 118:22-24

[9]I am probably over-simplifying, but I want to make sure you understand and don't reject me.

Prophecies of His Incarnation and Death
Other prophecies say,

"...A synagogue of sinners has encompassed Me; They pierced My hands and My feet."
Based on Psalm 22:16

"They surrounded Me like bees 'round the honeycomb." *Based on Psalm 118:12*

"They cast lots for My clothing." *Based on Psalm 22:18*

[13]These prophecies show He was destined to manifest in the flesh and suffer and die.

Prophecies of Israel
About Israel, the prophets said,

"Woe unto their soul, for they have counselled evil counsel against themselves saying, Let us bind the Just One, for He is unprofitable for us."
Isaiah 3:10 LXX

[15]Moses prophesied to them saying,

"Behold, these things saith the Lord God; enter into the good land which the Lord sware unto Abraham,

Epistle of Barnabas

Isaac, and Jacob, and inherit it, a land flowing with milk and honey." *Based on Exodus 33:1; Leviticus 20:24*

[16]Wisdom says we should learn about and completely trust Him who was manifested in the flesh, namely Jesus. [17]Man suffers in sin because he is from Adam, who was created out of the earth. [18]Why then did God say "into the good land, a land flowing with milk and honey?" [19]Blessed be our Lord, who has placed in us wisdom and understanding of His secrets. For the prophecy spoke about our Lord when He said,

"Who shall comprehend, save he that is wise and prudent and that loveth his Lord?"
Based on Hosea 14:9

The New Creation
[21]He has renewed us by the remission of our sins, and made us into new child-like souls, as if He was re-creating us. [22]Scripture records how the Father spoke to the Son about our creation,

"Let Us make man in Our image, according to Our likeness; and let them rule over beasts of the earth, the birds of the sky, and the fish of the sea... and God said 'be fruitful and multiply, and fill the earth'" *Based on Genesis 1:26,28*

[24]All this the Father spoke to His Son. Now I will show you how in these latter days He made us a new creation. [25]The Lord said He would make the last like the first; and this is why the prophet said, "enter into a land flowing with milk and honey and have dominion over it." [26]The Scripture also says of the new creations,

32

"I will take out from these, that is to say, from those whom the Spirit of the Lord foresaw, their stony hearts, and will put into them hearts of flesh."
Based on Ezekiel 11:19

[28]For He Himself was to be manifest in our flesh and dwell in us. The holy temple of the Lord is now our hearts. [29]Where does the Scripture say I should appear before the Lord my God, and be glorified?

"I will confess to Thee in the Church in the midst of my brethren; and I will praise Thee in the midst of the assembly of the saints."
Based on Psalms 22:22; 35:18; 149:1

[31]We then are the ones who are brought into the good land. But what does the milk and honey represent? [32]A child is kept alive by honey and milk. [33]So, in like manner, we are kept alive by faith in the promise and by the word, and shall rule over the earth.

Dominion in the Millennium
[34]For He said,

"Let them increase and rule over the fishes."
Based on Genesis 1:28

[35]Do we rule over the beasts, fishes, and birds now? [36]We must understand that to rule implies authority. [37]We cannot give commands or have complete control over them now. [38]But He tells us we will have it. [39]When we become perfect, we will inherit the covenant of the Lord!

Epistle of Barnabas

Commentary

Chapter 6 teaches that Jesus came to create a new nation of kings and priests. By building the church, He, Himself is the chief cornerstone. Israel rejected Him and had Him crucified so that everyone might be able to receive eternal life. We are now a new creation in Christ and have a godlike nature in addition to our sinful fleshly nature; and we have the guidance of the Holy Spirit in our lives. Ultimately, in the Millennium, we will have our resurrected, glorified bodies, with no pain or sin nature. Then we will be perfect, sinless, glorified, and have complete dominion as the Lord originally intended.

Paul describes Jesus as a type of Second Adam in Romans 5, so the concept is clearly biblical.

Chapter 6

Christians are New Creations in Christ

7
Types of Christ on Yom Kippur

[1]Understand and rejoice children, the Lord has predicted all things to us beforehand, so we can give thanks and praise Him. [2]If then the Son of God, who will judge the living and the dead, suffered that His stripes might give us life, we should understand He suffered for our sake. [3]Moreover, when He was crucified they gave Him vinegar and gall to drink. [4]The priests of the Temple prophetically foreshadowed this.

Yom Kippur Fast Commanded

[5]There is a commandment in Scripture that says,

> "Whosoever shall not observe the fast [of Yom Kippur] shall surely die" *Based on Leviticus 23:29*

[7]The Lord commanded this because He was about to offer His body as a sacrifice for sins, to fulfill the prophetic type of Isaac being offered on the altar.[i] [8]The Scripture also reveals a prophetic type based on the goat sacrificed on the Fast of Yom Kippur. [9]Look carefully at how it was eaten,

> "At the end of the Yom Kippur fast, let them eat the goat offered for their sins. Let all the priests alone eat the entrails unwashed with vinegar." *Based on an unknown source*

[11]Why? Because Christ knew when He would offer His flesh for the sins of His new people, He would be given

---

[i] See Genesis 22

gall and vinegar to drink. [12]Notice the priests, who are a type of Christ, eat this while the people are fasting in sackcloth and ashes, showing that it was necessary for Him to suffer for sinners.

The Two Goats
[13]God commanded on Yom Kippur, that two identical goats be offered to the high priest. The high priest will take one of them and offer it as a whole burnt-offering for sins. [14]What did he do with the other one? It was cursed. Understand how this was a type of Jesus. [15]It was spit upon, goaded, a scarlet wool cord was tied to its head, and it was cast into the wilderness. [16]At this point, a priest appointed for this task took the goat to a special place in the wilderness called Rachia. He then removed the scarlet cord and tied it to a shrub and cast the goat over a cliff. [17]The berries of this plant are normally bitter, but at that place when the goat is killed, the berries are made sweet. [18]Listen carefully to what this teaches us. One goat was for the altar and the other was accursed. [19]The accursed one was crowned with a scarlet cord. They will see Him on that day wearing a long scarlet robe around His flesh and say, "Is this not He who was rejected, spit upon, pierced, and crucified? Truly He is the Son of God!"

The Two Comings of the Messiah
[20]The goats are identical so they will understand there is only one Messiah, destined to come twice; once as the suffering Messiah and at His Second Coming, to rule as King Messiah. [21]The scarlet wool cord placed on the bush represents what the church must endure. Anyone wanting to take the wool had to endure being stuck by thorns. [22]Jesus taught us that whoever desired to see Him and attain to His kingdom must come though suffering and trials.

Commentary

Chapter 7 teaches the ritual of the Day of Atonement, or Yom Kippur, typologically shows Jesus would suffer and die on the cross, and that we will suffer for Him in this life. (This teaching is also found in Philippians 1:29 and Acts 14:22). It also teaches that there would be two comings of the Messiah. Some of the details given here are not found in Leviticus 16, but some are given in greater detail in the *Mishna, Moed, Yoma 6.*

The sacrifice of Isaac is a typological prophecy of Jesus. Isaac willingly submitted to his father Abraham to be sacrificed, and he may actually have been 33 years old, the same age as Jesus when He submitted to His father's will by dying on the cross. In this passage Abraham said, "God will provide Himself a sacrifice," meaning Jesus, who is God incarnate, would sacrifice Himself. Abraham also called the place where he offered his son, "Jehovah Jirah," which means, "the Lord will be seen." Abraham's sacrifice and Jesus' sacrifice took place on the very same mountain, Mount Moriah!

Chapter 7

8

The Red Heifer a Type of Christ

[1]What does the sacrifice of the red heifer[j] typify? [2]It was to be a whole burnt offering by the oldest of sinners and then young men were to gather its ashes, and put them into vessels and they also tied a piece of scarlet wool with hyssop on a stick. (Again see a type of the cross and scarlet wool). [3]This stick would be used by the young men to sprinkle the people one by one so that all of them may be cleansed from their sins. [4]Understand the typology of this rite. The calf represents Jesus, and the men who offer it are those who led Him for slaughter. Afterwards the men are no longer sinners but innocent children. [5]The young men who sprinkle the people represent the twelve who preached the forgiveness of sins and the purification of the heart. [6]At the beginning, the Lord gave the authority to preach the Gospel to the Twelve for a testimony to the twelve tribes of Israel. [7]Why then were there only three young men who sprinkled? For a testimony to Abraham, Isaac, and Jacob because these three received the covenant. [8]The wool on the stick represents that fact that the kingdom of Jesus was founded upon the cross; therefore they who believe in Him will live forever. [9]The hyssop and wool were put together to signify that in His kingdom the days will be evil and polluted days, in which, however, we will be saved; and because anyone who had a physical disease was cured by the cleansing efficacy of hyssop. [10]These things are clear to us, but they are obscure to the Jews, because they no longer hear the voice of the Lord.

---

[j] See Numbers 19

Chapter 8

Commentary

In Hebrews 9, Paul also wrote that the Red Heifer ceremony pointed to Christ. John 19:29 revealed that hyssop soaked in vinegar was given to Jesus.

The Red Heifer was a whole burnt offering; its ashes were taken to use for purification rites. A small amount of the ashes were sprinkled on large water pots to create holy water. This water of purification would then be used to sprinkle on people to make them ceremonially clean. We see these same water pots in John 2 where Jesus used them to change the water to wine.

9

The Typology of Circumcision

[1]He also speaks about circumcising our ears and hearts. [2]The Prophet said,

> "In the hearing of the ear they obey Me."
> *Psalm 17:44 LXX*

[3]And again he said,

> "Those who are afar off will hear and they will know what I have done." *Based on Isaiah 33:13*

[4]And again,

> "'Be circumcised in your hearts', says the Lord."
> *Based on Jeremiah 4:4*

[5]And again the Spirit of God prophesies, saying,

> "Hear O Israel! For thus says the Lord your God. Whoever would live forever, let him hear the voice of My Son." *Unknown*

[6]Again He said,

> "Hear, O heaven, and give ear, O earth, for the Lord hath spoken these things for a testimony."
> *Based on Isaiah 1:2*

[7]These are proof. And again He says,

"Hear the word of the Lord, you rulers of this people." *Unknown*

[8]And again He says,

"Hear, you children, the voice of one crying in the wilderness." *Based on Isaiah 40:3*

[9]Therefore He circumcised our ears that we might hear His word and believe. For the circumcision they trusted in has been abolished. [10]He declared that true circumcision was not of the flesh; but they misunderstood because an evil one deceived them. [11]I see a new commandment where the Lord said to them,

"These things says the Lord your God; 'Sow not among thorns, but circumcise yourselves to the Lord.'" *Based on Jeremiah 4:3-4*

[12]Why does He say,

"Circumcise the stubbornness of your heart, and harden not your neck" *Based on Deuteronomy 10:16*

[13]Again the Lord says,

"'Behold,' says the Lord, 'all the nations are uncircumcised in the flesh, but this people are uncircumcised in heart.'" *Based on Jeremiah 9:25-26*

[14]You might say, 'but the people of Israel were physically circumcised for a sign.' [15]True, but every Syrian, and Arabian, including all their idolatrous priests, practice circumcision. Are they all part of the covenant? [16]Don't you know that even the Egyptians are part of the circumcision? [17]Please, dear children, understand the

whole teaching completely. [18]Abraham, who was the first appointed with circumcision, looked forward in the spirit to Jesus, while practicing that rite because he received the teaching of the Three-Fold Witness.

Addition or Corruption

[19]The Scripture says Abraham circumcised ten, and eight, and three hundred men of his household (Genesis 14:14; 17:13). [20]Why is the eighteen written first, then the three hundred? The "I" stands for ten, "H" stands for eight, and the "T" stands for three hundred. The letters "IH" then are the first two letters of the name Jesus, and hence an acronym for Jesus. The "T" is a symbol of the cross. [21]He who has put the engrafted gift of his doctrine within us, knows that I never taught to anyone a more certain truth; but I trust that you are worthy of it.

Commentary

Physical circumcision represented the removal of hardness of the soul in true repentance. Satan misled the Jews into thinking it was a health issue and they followed the command blindly, never understanding the true meaning. They did the same thing with the weekly Sabbath, and today some Christians do the same thing with baptism.

The Apostle Paul agreed with Barnabas that circumcision is a typological prophecy when he taught true circumcision is the putting off of the sinful nature, not the fleshly sign.

> "In whom also ye are circumcised with the circumcision made without hands, in putting off the body of the sins of the flesh by the circumcision of Christ" Colossians 2:11 KJV

The comment about Abraham receiving the Three-Fold Witness is referring back to chapter one: namely Eternal life, Creation, and Prophecy. Abraham was taught about the Creation and Fall of man and everyone's need for a savior. He knew about the prophecies of a coming Redeemer. God actually appeared to him and gave him a prophecy about his descendants being enslaved; and then, after 400 years, inheriting the Land of Canaan. According to old Hebrew historical records, the Israelites knew the approximate date for the Exodus because they took Abraham's teaching about the prophecy seriously. Abraham knew well, and taught to this descendants, the need for a Savior, creationism, and to expect the prophecies to literally occur when they were predicted to. See the last three chapters for details and the books *Ancient Prophecies Revealed, Ancient Post-Flood History,* and *Ancient Church Fathers* for more information.

Note verses 19-21. The ancient church fathers taught we should stay away from Bible codes. The "I" and "H" do not correspond to 8 and 10 but are the first two letters in Jesus' name. This is most likely an addition by some Gnostic cult trying to add its doctrine to the widely accepted text.

10
The Typology of Jewish Food Laws

Additions of Moses

[1]Why did Moses say, you can't eat swine, eagles, hawks, crows, or fish that don't have fins and scales? [2]These animals symbolically represent three concepts. Moses said in Deuteronomy;

> "I will give *my* ordinances to this people."
> *Based on Deuteronomy 4:1*

[4]Didn't God command the Israelites not to eat these things? Yes He did, but Moses was allowed to add to the Covenant to teach spiritual truths.

What the Forbidden Animals Typify

[5]Swine are animals that come when they are called only if they are hungry. If they are full, they ignore their master. They represent men who come to God when in a crisis but have no time for God when they are content. We should avoid men like this. [6]The eagle, hawk, kite, and crow are animals that don't hunt and kill their own food but steal it from other birds. They are forbidden foods because they represent laziness[k] and coveting, resulting in sins like robbery and rape. [7]The lamprey, polypus, and cuttlefish are animals that swim at the bottom of the deep, never coming to the surface. These teach us not to consort with, nor become like, men who are ungodly, those already condemned to death. [8]The hare is an animal that multiplies rapidly and with every conception it has a

---

[k] The unruly of 2 Thessalonians 3:6-18.

different mate.[1] They represent chambering [living together without lawful marriage], adultery, polygamy [either many wives at the same time or though divorce and remarriage], incest, and fornication in general. [9]The hyena is an animal that may look male or female depending on its age. They represent homosexuality [sodomy], bisexuality, and pedophilia. Don't even resemble such people [in cross-dressing or in mannerisms, etc.]. [10]The weasel is an animal that begins its mating ritual with its mouth. It spiritually signifies people who perform oral sex. Avoid all such people, both men and women.

The Misunderstanding
[11]When Moses spoke of eating these foods, he was actually conveying a typological prophecy based on the principle of the Three-Fold Witness, but the Jews never understood this, assuming they were only for health reasons.

King David
[12]King David demonstrated that he understood the principle of the Three-Fold Witness when he said,

"How blessed is the man who does not walk in the counsel of the ungodly" *Based on Psalm 1:1*

[14]These are like the fishes that go in darkness to the depths of the sea.

"Nor stand in the way of sinners" *Psalm 1:1*

[16]Those who pretend to fear the Lord yet sin like swine;

---

[1] Dogs are also known to represent promiscuity.

"Nor sit in the seat of scoffers!" *Psalm 1:1*

[18]Scoffers are like those birds that sit and watch for those they can devour. [19]Make sure you fully grasp this spiritual teaching of the Jewish food laws.

What the Clean Animals Typify
[20]On the positive side, what did Moses mean when he said you should eat animals that have cloven hooves and chew their cud? [21]An animal that chews its cud receives food from its master and is always glad to see him, meaning we should fellowship with men who are glad to constantly study God's word in order to fully understand and obey all it contains. [22]An animal that is cloven hoofed represents the righteous who walks in this world but is not a part of it, because he constantly looks forward to the Rapture.

The Holy Spirit Is Required To Understand
[23]See how well Moses legislated. [24]Was it possible for the Jews to understand what these food laws were really for? [25]We truly understand these commandments only because the Lord has circumcised our ears and hearts with the Holy Spirit.

Commentary

This chapter gives us the information that even though the Jewish food laws may have been partly given to the Jews for health reasons, they were also typological prophecies about how God expects us to live our lives, morally.

Since we see Barnabas in Galatians 2 standing for Jewish food laws with Peter, and then corrected by the Apostle Paul, it makes perfect sense that this chapter be included in his work.

There are numerous examples of God allowing Moses to add laws of his own making to govern the Jews. Some were even used to teach typological prophecy. At one time Moses was supposed to strike a rock (symbolizing Christ smitten for our sins); and the second time, in Numbers 20:8, Moses was supposed to *speak* to the rock, but he hit it again (this would symbolize Jesus begin crucified twice, which is not possible). Because Moses broke the pattern of a typological prophecy, God punished him by not allowing him to enter the Promised Land. The same thing happened with Nadab and Abihu in Leviticus 10:1-2, where they offered strange fire to the Lord. This would symbolize a way to God would be possible apart from Christ. Since this could not be taught, Nadab and Abihu were killed.

The first century church decided Jewish food laws and circumcision were not necessary for Gentile Christians, according to Acts 15. After praying for the Holy Spirit's guidance in that situation they declared…

"It seemed good to the Holy Ghost, and to us, to lay upon you no greater burden than these necessary things; That ye abstain from meats offered to idols, and from blood, and from things strangled, and from fornication: from which if ye keep yourselves, ye shall do well. Fare ye well." *Acts 15:28-29 KJV*

11
Baptism Typified in the Old Testament

[1]Let us inquire as to whether the Lord took care to reveal anything beforehand concerning water baptism and the cross. [2]About the water, it is written that the people of Israel would not receive baptism for the remission of sins, but would institute another kind baptism for themselves that cannot remit sin. [3]For the prophets said,

> "Be astonished, O Heaven! And let the earth tremble at it, because this people have done two great and evil things: they have left Me, the fountain of living water, and have dug for themselves broken cisterns that can hold no water." *Based on Jeremiah 2:12, 13*

> "Is My holy mountain of Sinai a desert rock? For you will be as baby birds, which fly away when the nest is removed." *Based on Isaiah 16:1,2*

> "I will go before you and make level the mountains, and will break the brazen gates, and cut in pieces the iron bars; and I will give you the secret, hidden, invisible treasures, that they may know that I am the Lord God." *Based on Isaiah 45:2,3*

> "He shall dwell in a lofty cave of the strong rock... His water is sure; you will see the King in His glory, and your soul will meditate on the fear of the Lord." *Based on Isaiah 33:16-18*

> "He that does these things will be like a tree, planted by the currents of water, which will give its fruit in its season. Its leaf will not wither, and whatever he

does will prosper. It is not so for the wicked; they are as the dust which the wind scatters away from the face of the earth. Therefore the ungodly will not rise up in judgment, nor do sinners sit in the counsel of the just; for the Lord knows the way of the righteous, but the way of the ungodly will perish."
Based on Psalm 1:3-6

[8]Understand how He has connected the cross and water.

True Baptism
[9]These words imply that you will be blessed if you place your trust in the cross by being baptized in water. God will give them their reward in due time. [10]When the Scripture says "their leaves will not fade" is means every word that comes out of your mouth will tend to bring about conversion by bringing hope to many. [11]Another prophet says,

"The land of Jacob was praised above every land."
Based on Zephaniah 3:19

[12]This referred to the vessel of His Spirit (the body of Christ), which He shall glorify. What else did he say?

"there was a river flowing on the right, and beautiful trees grew out of it, and whosoever shall eat of them shall live forever." *Based on Ezekiel 47:12*

[14]The significance of this is that we go down into the baptismal water full of sins and completely defiled, but come up bearing fruit in our heart and having hope in Jesus in the Spirit. [15]And where he says "whoever will eat them will live forever," he means whoever will listen to these things and believe, will live forever.

Commentary

In 1 Peter 3:20-21, Peter reveals that Noah is a type of the Church. Noah's going though the Flood and coming up in a new world is like a new believer being baptized into a new eternal life. Other ancient church fathers have commented that the Israelites' going down into the Red Sea and coming back up alive was a type of baptism.

Chapter 11

Water Baptism Typifies the New Birth

12
The Cross Typified in the Old Testament

¹In like manner He points to the cross of Christ when the prophet asked, "when shall these things be fulfilled?" The Lord answered,

> "When a tree shall be bent and stand upright, and when blood will flow from a tree." *Unknown Quote*

³Another example of the cross and Him who would be crucified, is when Israel was losing a battle because God wanted to teach them death comes on them because of their sins.

The Sign of the Cross
⁴The Holy Spirit moved Moses to represent the sign of the cross because, unless they put their trust in Christ who would suffer upon it, they would be overcome forever. ⁵So Moses piled up armor upon armor in the midst of the hill, stood on it in order to be seen by all and stretched forth his hands and Israel obtained the victory. ⁶But no sooner did he put down his hands, then they began losing the battle again.ᵐ God did this to show them they could not be saved unless they put their trust in Him. In another place a prophet declared,

> "All day long I have stretched out My hands to an unbelieving people, and who speak against My righteous way." *Based on Isaiah 65:2; Romans 10:21*

ᵐ See Exodus 17:8-12

[8]Moses made another typological prophecy about Jesus, His suffering on the cross, and that the Jews would seek to destroy Him even though He was the only way to eternal life. [9]Since Eve transgressed through the serpent, the Lord caused deadly serpents to attack the Israelites. [10]This should have taught them their own sins are what cause death. Even though God instructed the Israelites not to create graven images, He instructed Moses to create a brazen serpent[n] to foreshadow Jesus Christ. [11]Moses placed the brazen serpent on a pole and instructed the people that if anyone who was bitten would come to the brazen serpent and truly repent, they would be healed.

Joshua Son of Nun
[12]Another typological prophecy of the glory of Jesus is when Moses named Joshua son of Nun as the people's new leader. [In Greek, Joshua means "Jesus" and Nun means "fish."] He prophetically said the people should "listen to him alone." [13]This was another way that the Father revealed all things about His son Jesus. After naming Joshua son of Nun as leader, Moses told him to spy out the land and to

> "Take a book in your hands, and write what the Lord says, how the son of God shall cut out by the roots all the house of Amalek in the last days."
> *Based on Exodus 17:14*

[15]Here Jesus is again manifested typologically and in the flesh, not as a Son of Man, but as the Son of God!

Son of David
[16]Since it was prophesied that the Christ would be a descendant of David, David wrote,

---

[n] See Numbers 21:6-9 and John 3:14-18

> "The Lord said to my Lord, sit at My right hand until I make Your enemies Your footstool."
> *Psalm 110:1*

[18]Again Isaiah says the same,

> "The Lord said to Christ my Lord, I have laid hold on His right hand, that the nations should obey before Him, and I will break the strength of kings."
> *Unknown Quote*

[20]See how both David and Isaiah call Him "Lord," and not "son."

Commentary

Many ancient church fathers, including Irenaeus, Justin Martyr, and John Chrysostom, taught that Moses' upraised arms formed a cross and this was a typological prophecy that victory over sin and death would be through the cross of Christ.

The first century Christians used the Greek word for fish, ΙΧΘΥΣ, as an acrostic. Each letter in the word is the first letter for the sentence "Jesus Christ God's Son Savior." In places where Christians would gather secretly, the symbol of the fish could be found carved on the walls and floors.

This chapter teaches us that since the Hebrew word for Joshua means "Jesus," and Nun means "fish," that the full name of Joshua son of Nun is yet another typological prophecy of Jesus being the Messiah, God's Son, and the savior of mankind.

The last comment about verse 15 repeats what Paul said,

> "God was manifest in the flesh, justified in the Spirit, seen of angels, preached unto the Gentiles, believed on in the world, received up into glory." *1 Timothy 3:16 KJV*

The Fish Was An Ancinet Symbol Of The Christains

13

Christians Are the Heirs of the Covenant

Another People Through Isaac

[1]We must look carefully at the Scriptures to see if the covenant was designed for only ethnic Israelites or for believers in the Messiah, for Jews or Christians. [2]Notice what Scripture says about Israel; Isaac prayed for his barren wife, Rebekah. [3]When Rebekah found out the Lord answered his prayer; she went to inquire of the Lord about her pregnancy. [4]The Lord said to her,

> "Two nations are in your womb, and two peoples in your belly; and the one people shall surpass the other, and the elder shall serve the younger."
> *Based on Genesis 25:23*

[5]You need to understand what Isaac and Rebekah represent and why one of their children would rule over the other.

Another People through Joseph

[6]In another prophecy, Jacob shows the same kind of typology when he spoke to his son Joseph. Jacob said,

> "Behold the Lord has not deprived me of your presence; bring me your sons, so I may bless them."
> *Based on Genesis 48:9-11*

[8]Joseph brought Ephraim and Manasseh to Jacob. Joseph wanted his eldest son to be blessed, so he placed Manasseh at the right hand of Jacob. [9]Jacob, by the Spirit, foresaw in type a people who were to come. What does the Scripture say?

"Jacob crossed his hands, and placed his right hand on the head of Ephraim, the second and younger, and blessed him. But Joseph said unto Jacob, 'Transfer your right hand to the head of Manasseh, for he is my first-born son. Jacob said to Joseph, I know it, my son, I know it; but the greater will serve the lesser.'" *Based on Genesis 48:14,17-19*

[11]So you can see which people are appointed heirs of the covenant.

Another People through Abraham
[12]Look at one more Scripture and you should completely understand. God also showed us the coming Christian church though father Abraham. [13]When Abraham believed God and that belief alone was accredited to him for righteousness, what did God say to Him?

"Behold, I have made you the father of those nations who believe in the Lord yet remain uncircumcised." *Based on an unknown reference*

Epistle of Barnabas

Commentary

Compare verse 4 with Paul's teaching about Isaac and Rebekah and the coming church in Romans 9:5, 6-8, 10-16.

Isaac and Rebekah, like Abraham and Sarah, were obedient to God and had children of promise. One of the children of promise would reject the things of God and one would accept them. They are a typological prophecy of the Jews rejecting the Messiah and the church inheriting the blessings of the Messiah.

Many of the ancient church fathers taught that when Jacob crossed his hands and blessed Ephraim and Manasseh, it was yet another symbol of the cross of Christ.

Verses 12-14 state the same concept recorded by Paul in Romans 4:1-5. Abraham is the father of believing Gentiles who remain uncircumcised because he received the blessing of God while he was still uncircumcised.

In Galatians 4:21-31, Paul taught that God made Sarah's and Hagar's situation a typological prophecy of the two covenants.

The Old Covenant Prophesied the New

14

The New Covenant

[1]Let us now inquire if the Lord actually gave the new covenant which He swore to our fathers that He would give to the people. [2]He indeed gave it, but they were not worthy to receive it because of their sins. [3]The prophet said,

> "And Moses was fasting forty days and forty nights on Mount Sinai, that he might receive the testament of the Lord for the people... And he received from the Lord two tables, written in the Spirit by the finger of the hand of the Lord."
> *Based on Exodus 24:18; 31:18*

[4]Moses received them and carried them down to give to the people. The Lord then said to Moses,

> "Moses, Moses, go down quickly; for your people have sinned, whom you brought out of the land of Egypt." *Based on Exodus 32:7*

[6]Moses understood that the Israelites had made molten images and he threw down the tablets of the covenant of the Lord and broke them into pieces. [7]Moses received them, but the people were not worthy. How did we receive them? [8]Moses received it when he was a servant[o], but the Lord Himself gave it to us, as the people of the inheritance, by suffering for us. [9]He was manifest in order that at the same time they should fill up the measure of their sins; and that we, being made heirs by Him, should

---

[o] See Hebrews 3:5

receive the covenant of the Lord Jesus. [10]By His personal incarnation He was prepared for this purpose of redeeming our hearts from the darkness, which had already brought us death through the iniquity of deceit, and established the covenant with us by His word. [11]It is written how the Father charged Him to deliver us from darkness and prepare for Himself a holy people. The prophet said,

"I, the Lord your God, have called You in righteousness, and I will hold Your hand and strengthen You. And give You as a covenant of the people, for a light to the Gentiles, to open the eyes of the blind, to free the prisoners from the prison, and them that sit in darkness out of the prison house." *Based on Isaiah 42:6-7*

[13]We know now why we were redeemed. Again the prophet said,

"'Behold, I have assigned you to be a light to the Gentiles for salvation to all the ends of the earth,' says the Lord your God who has redeemed you." *Based on Isaiah 49:6*

"The spirit of the Lord is upon Me, because He has anointed Me; He has sent me to preach the gospel to the humble, to heal the broken-hearted, to preach deliverance to the captives and recovery of sight to the blind[p], to proclaim the acceptable year of the Lord and the day of recompense, and to comfort all that mourn." *Based on Isaiah 61:1-2*

---

[p] See Luke 4:17-21

Commentary

The main idea of this chapter is that the covenant between God and the Jews was broken. Now the covenant is for all who trust in the Messiah, both Jews and Gentiles. This idea is taught constantly in the New Testament.

It gives the idea that Moses' breaking the laws on Mount Sinai was a typological prophecy of the coming of the new covenant. One that Jeremiah describes,

> "But this shall be the covenant that I will make with the house of Israel; After those days, saith the LORD, I will put my law in their inward parts, and write it in their hearts; and will be their God, and they shall be my people." *Jeremiah 31:33 KJV*

Paul acknowledged God caused Moses to act strangely in order to perform typological prophecies in other situations as well. When Moses struck the rock, that action typified Christ (See 1 Corinthians 10:3). And when he put the veil over his face, it typified the coming new covenant (See 2 Corinthians 3:7-14).

The New Covenant

15
The Sabbath Typifies the Millennium

[1]God spoke to Moses face to face on Mount Sinai about the Sabbath. The Sabbath law is also written in the Ten Commandments. [2]You are to hold sacred the Sabbath with pure hands and a clean heart. [3]In one place He says,

> "If My sons observe the Sabbath, then I will bestow My mercy upon them." *Based on Leviticus 26:2-5*

[4]The Sabbath is mentioned at the very beginning of Creation,

> "In six days God made all the works of His hands and when He had finished, He rested on the seventh day and sanctified it." *Based on Genesis 2:2-3*

[5]What this teaches us is this: God ended all of creation in six days. This is a typological prophecy showing that in six thousand years the Lord will bring all things to an end; for a day is like a thousand years with Him. [6]He Himself testified, saying,

> "One day with the Lord is as a thousand years."
> *Based on 2 Peter 3:8*

Six Thousand Years of Human History
[7]Therefore, children, in six days, or in six thousand years, all the prophecies will be fulfilled[q]. [8]Then it says, He rested on the seventh day. This signifies at the Second Coming of our Lord Jesus, He will destroy the Antichrist,

---

[q] See 2 Peter 3:8-9

judge the ungodly, and change the sun, moon, and stars.
[9]Then He will truly rest during the Millennial reign,
which is the seventh day. [10]He further said,

> "You shall keep it holy with clean hands and a pure
> heart." *Based on Psalm 24:4*

No One Can Truly Keep the Sabbath

[11]If anyone thinks he can keep the weekly Sabbath now
with a pure heart, he is deceiving himself. [12]We will
indeed be able to rest and sanctify it when we are
justified, receive our glorified bodies which no longer
have a sin nature, and all things have been made new by
our Lord. [13]We will then be able to sanctify it because we
ourselves will be completely sanctified. [14]Finally, when
He said to them,

> "I can't stand your new moons and Sabbaths."
> *Based on Isaiah 1:13*

[15]Do you see what He means? He said,

> "Your present Sabbaths are not acceptable to me;
> only the one I have ordained, namely, the rest that I
> will give on the eighth day, which will be the
> beginning of the eternal kingdom."
> *Based on an unknown reference*

[16]This is why we celebrate the eighth day with gladness,
in which Jesus rose from the dead, and appeared to many
people, then ascended to heaven.

Epistle of Barnabas

Commentary
Psalm 24 is thought by many of the ancient church fathers and prophecy students alike, to be a riddle referring to the Millennium.

Many ancient church fathers taught the Second Coming would be at the end of 6,000 years of human history, or 2,000 years after Christ's First Coming. These include: Barnabas, Irenaeus, Hippolytus, Theophilus, Aviricius Marcellus, Cyprian, Commodianus, Lactantius, Bardesan, and others.

In the ritual of Yom Kippur, there is a day called "Shimini Azteret" or the eighth conclusion. This is briefly mentioned in Leviticus 23:30-39. This part of the ritual teaches about the beginning of eternity after the Millennial reign. It is referred to as the "Olam HaBah," or eternal Kingdom.

The Prophet of Old

used Typological Prophecies

16
The Spiritual Temple of God

¹I still need to speak to you concerning the Temple. The wretched men, being deceived, put their trust in a building instead of God who created them. ²They began to worship God in His Temple like the Gentiles worship their gods. ³What did the Lord say when He abolished His Temple?

> "'Who has meted out heaven with a span, and the earth with his palm? Have not I?' says the Lord… 'Heaven is My throne, and the earth My footstool: what kind of house will you build for Me, or what is the place of My rest?'" *Based on Isaiah 40:12; 66:1*

⁵You can perceive that their hope is vain. Furthermore the Lord said,

> "Behold, they who destroy this temple, even they will again build it up once more."
> *Based on an unknown reference*

⁷This prophecy was fulfilled because the Jews went to war against their enemy. But even though they are now no more than servants to Rome, they will return and rebuild the Temple. ⁸It was revealed that the city of Jerusalem, the Temple, and the people of Israel were to be given up. ⁹For the Scripture said,

> "It will come to pass in the last days, that the Lord will deliver up the sheep of His pasture, and their fold and tower, to destruction."
> *Based on an unknown reference*

¹⁰Since exactly what the Lord had prophesied has come to pass, let us inquire whether or not a Temple of God still exists. ¹¹It does exist, for He Himself declared that He would both make and perfect it. ¹²It is written,

> "It shall come to pass, when the week is being completed, the Temple of God shall be built gloriously in the name of the Lord."
> *Based on Daniel 9:24,25; Haggai 2:9*

¹³I find then that there is currently a Temple. Understand how it is built in the name of the Lord. ¹⁴Before we believed in God, the habitation of our heart was corrupt and weak, like a temple built by pagan hands; a demonic temple full of idolatry and everything contrary to God. ¹⁵How is the Temple built in the name of the Lord and for His glory? ¹⁶When we received the remission of sins, and put our trust in the Name [HaShem], we became new creatures in Christ, recreated as it were from the beginning. ¹⁷Therefore, God truly dwells in us as a habitation. ¹⁸We know this by the word of His faith, the calling of His promise, the wisdom of His righteous judgments, and the commands of His teaching. ¹⁹He prophesies in us and He dwells in us. He opened the door to the Temple for us who were in bondage to sin and death. ²⁰We become an incorruptible temple by the voice of wisdom granting us repentance. ²¹Every saved person who listens to a man inspired by the Holy Spirit takes away something different. These people are truly in the spiritual Temple built up by the Lord.

Epistle of Barnabas

Commentary

Notice verse 6 shows the Jews were the cause of the destruction of the Temple, and upon their return, they will rebuild it. This indicates Barnabas believed in the Micah 5 prophecy and expected the Jews to return and rebuild their Temple before the Second Coming. The Jews returned to their land in AD 1948, took control of the Temple Mount in AD 1967, and to date the Temple has yet to be rebuilt (See *Ancient Prophecies Revealed* for full details). The comment that the destruction of the Temple has occurred proves this epistle was written after AD 70.

Christians are the currently the Temple in the truest sense of the word. True believers have always been the true Temple. In the midst of Daniel's 70th week, the Jews will rebuild the Temple. Then all of Israel will accept the Messiah and the Temple will truly receive God's glory. After its desecration, the Messiah will return and build the Millennial Temple. In both of these cases the true Temple will still be the true worshipers. For example, the two witnesses of Revelation are believers in the Messiah when other priests may not be. The Lord has always had a people.

Believers have always been

the true Temple

17
Salvation and Prophecy

[1]It is my desire, as far as possible, to simply declare to you all the things pertaining to salvation. [2]If I spoke further to you about the immediate and future prophecies, you would not yet understand them because they are hidden as riddles. So much for them.

18
The Two Ways

[1]Let us now go on to another kind of knowledge and doctrine. [2]There are two ways of knowledge and power, the one is of light and the other is of darkness. There is a great difference between the two ways. [3]For over the one are God's angels, who teach the way of light, and over the other are Satan's angels. [4]The Lord our God rules over the one throughout all eternity; and Satan, the prince of the air, rules over the present time of iniquity.

Commentary

Now that we have seen another 2,000 years of history pass, we can begin to unravel the prophecies "hidden in riddles." As of AD 2010, over 50 biblical prophecies have been fulfilled since Israel has been revived as a nation. See the last three chapters of this book and *Ancient Prophecies Revealed* for more information.

Now more than ever, it is important to remain faithful to the teachings of Scripture, and to remain moral. To this end Barnabas gives us his list of do's and don'ts.

19
The Way of Light

[1]The way of light is this: if anyone desires to attain to eternal life, he must be zealous of his works. [2]The knowledge of how to walk in the light is this: you must love and honor God, your Creator, and glorify Jesus who redeemed you from death. [3]Be simple in heart and rich in spirit; don't join those who walk in the way of death. [4]Hate everything that is not pleasing to God, especially hypocrisy, and never neglect any of the commandments of our Lord Jesus. [5]Don't exalt yourself, but instead be humble. [6]Don't accept glory for yourself, nor form evil plans against your neighbor. [7]Don't be arrogant[r], fornicate, commit adultery, or corrupt boys [homosexual pedophilia, sodomy]. [8]Don't proclaim the Gospel while living a life of corrupt morals. [9]Don't show partiality, but reprove everyone for transgression. [10]You must be gentle, quiet, and live your life by these words. [11]Don't hold a grudge, doubt the prophecies, or take the Lord's name in vain, but love your neighbor more than your own soul. [12]Don't murder a child by abortion, or kill the child after its birth. [13]Don't withhold corporal punishment from your children, but teach them the fear of God while they are young. [14]Don't covet, be greedy, or walk in pride; but be humble and righteous. [15]View all the trials you experience as God-ordained and you will be blessed. [16]Don't be double-minded or double-tongued, but obey your masters[s] as you would God, with meekness and fear. [17]Don't bitterly command your bondservant or maidservant who

---

[r] Arrogant can mean being too self-confident by not relying on God.
[s] A master is anyone in a position of authority: your boss at work, your pastor, husband, policeman, or government official.

trusts in the same God as you, because they might cease to fear God who is over you both; because He didn't come to call men who looked righteous, but whomever the Spirit had prepared. [18]Share everything with your neighbor, for nothing is truly your own. If you are fellow-partakers in the imperishable, why aren't you in the perishable? [19]Don't be quick to speak, for the mouth is a deathtrap. [20]Strive to keep your soul pure. Don't constantly take, but refuse to give. [21]You must love, like the apple of your eye, everyone who speaks to you the word of the Lord. [22]Constantly remind yourselves the Day of Judgment is coming. Every day seek other saints either to study the word, (exhorting each other and finding new ways to share the Gospel) or work with your hands to help the poor, that your sins may be forgiven you. [23]Don't hesitate to give, or murmur when giving, knowing God will take care of you. [24]Carefully guard and preserve the Scriptures; neither add to, nor take away from them. [25]Hate Satan, judge righteously, and don't create a division; but make peace between adversaries. [26]Confess your sins and don't go to prayer with an evil conscience. This is the way of light.

Commentary
Barnabas made it very clear that abortion is murder, and homosexuality is a form of fornication.

20
The Way of Darkness

[1]The way of darkness is crooked and completely cursed. It is the way of eternal death and punishment. Those who walk in darkness embrace things that destroy their own souls. [2]These are: idolatry, self-confidence [apart from God], the pride of power, hypocrisy, double-mindedness, adultery, murder, robbery, rape, pride, transgression, deceit, malice, stubbornness, sorcery, magic, greed, and the lack of the fear of God. [3]Those who walk in darkness persecute the good, hate the truth, love lies, don't know the reward of the righteous, nor adhere to anything that is good or righteous. [4]They pay no attention to the widow or orphan, but spend wakeful nights not in the fear of God, but in the pursuit of vice. [5]They are neither gentle nor patient, but they love vanity and constantly seek a reward. [6]They have no compassion for the poor, nor help for those who are burdened and oppressed. [7]They are prone to slander and have no knowledge of their maker. [8]They murder children [abortion and infanticide], corrupt the creatures of God [homosexuality], turn away from the poor, and oppress the afflicted. [9]They are advocates of the rich, unjust judges of the poor, and are all together sinful.

Commentary

Barnabas makes it clear that having no knowledge of God or Jesus is a sin. Also listed is sorcery, which biblically is any form of meditation that places you in an altered state of consciousness. See *Ancient Paganism* for a complete discussion on sorcery.

21
The Conclusion

[1]It is essentially necessary then, that we learn, practice, and share the Three-Fold Witness ordained by God, namely, the facts about eternal life, creation, and prophecy. [2]Whoever practices these things will be glorified in God's kingdom; but whoever chooses the opposite will perish. [3]For this reason there will be both a resurrection and a retribution. [4]I implore you elders, heed my advice, seek fellowship with obedient Christians, but avoid the disobedient.[t] For the Day of the Lord will come, when His fiery judgment will melt away the elements and the evil one will be destroyed.[u] The Lord will come with His reward. [5]Once more I warn you, do away with all hypocrisy, by making sure that both you and those around you know and follow the precepts taught in the Scriptures. [6]I pray that our God, who is Lord over all the earth, give you wisdom, knowledge, discernment, complete understanding of His word, and patience, so that you come to know God's ways. [7]Diligently seek God's will for your life, and do everything in your power to make it happen, so you will escape the judgment in the Day of the Lord. [8]Remember me as you follow the teaching in this epistle that my desire be granted in watching you grow in the Lord. [9]I beg you, as long as you live, don't fail in any of these things. Constantly seek after them, and fulfill every command, for these things are proper and have to be done. [10]This is why I was anxious to write to you that I might encourage you. Farewell children of love and peace. The Lord of glory and grace be with your spirit. Amen.

---

[t] See 1 Corinthins 5:9-13
[u] See 2 Peter 3:10

Commentary
Again we are told to make sure we fully understand the Three-Fold Witness. The next three chapters are included to introduce to the reader ways we can, in our time, witness to others about eternal life, creationism, and prophecy.

The Three-Fold Witness

Eternal Life

The first part of the Three-fold Witness is that a mature Christian must be able to lead someone to the Lord. We must be able to show the plan of salvation from Scripture. One of the easiest ways to accomplish this is by using what is called the "Roman Road." Using just the book of Romans, explain that Adam and Eve were created sinless; but, the result of the Fall was that all of their descendants, both you and me, were born with a sin nature that causes us to commit sin.

> "For all have sinned, and come short of the glory of God;" *Romans 3:23 KJV*

Since every single human being has sinned, we are destined for hell, and there is nothing we can do by ourselves to change that.

> "For the wages of sin is death;" *Romans 6:23a KJV*

But the good news is that Jesus Christ paid for our sins by becoming human and dying on the cross.

> "but the gift of God is eternal life through Jesus Christ our Lord." *Romans 6:23b KJV*

Jesus loved us so much that He paid for our sins while we were still separated from Him.

> "But God commendeth his love toward us, in that, while we were yet sinners, Christ died for us." *Romans 5:8 KJV*

Everyone who believes and accepts what Jesus did for them becomes a Christian. We simply pray and ask Him to forgive us for our sins and begin to learn all the truths taught in the Scripture.

> "For whosoever shall call upon the name of the Lord shall be saved." *Romans 10:13 KJV*

We must believe tht Jesus is "Lord" or God Incarnate, the second person of the Trinity, and that He not only died but literally resurrected three days after His death and burial.

If we not only believe, but testify that we strongly hold to this faith and why we do so, then we will truly be saved. We will spend eternity with God and never spend once second in hell.

> "That if thou shalt confess with thy mouth the Lord Jesus, and shalt believe in thine heart that God hath raised him from the dead, thou shalt be saved. For with the heart man believeth unto righteousness; and with the mouth confession is made unto salvation." *Romans 10:9-10 KJV*

Creation History

Barnabas states the second of the Three-Fold Witness was to be able to explain Creation history. Many of the ancient church fathers taught that in the end times when the apostasy of the church was complete, the church itself would reject the teaching of Creation by saying Genesis was a myth. The apostate church would begin to teach the Pagan concept of evolution. The apostle Peter basically said the same thing,

> "Knowing this first, that there shall come in the last days scoffers, walking after their own lusts, And saying, Where is the promise of his coming? for since the fathers fell asleep, all things continue as they were from the beginning of the creation. For this they willingly are ignorant of, that by the word of God the heavens were of old, and the earth standing out of the water and in the water: Whereby the world that then was, being overflowed with water, perished: But the heavens and the earth, which are now, by the same word are kept in store, reserved unto fire against the day of judgment and perdition of ungodly men." *2 Peter 3:4-7 KJV*

Notice Peter said the end time scoffing church would be *willingly* ignorant of the Flood and the Second Coming prophecies. They do this by denying the inspiration of Scripture, saying the historical information recorded in Genesis is a myth; in which case, there was no Fall, and we do not need a savior. Today the forming apostate church rejects biblical creationism for the teaching of evolution. Most of these churches do not believe in premillennialism either, just as the Apostle Peter predicted!

In Barnabas' eyes, a mature Christian should not only be able to lead someone to the Lord Jesus and disciple them, but will also teach all new converts the facts of Creation and to guard against the lie of evolution.

To this end, many Christians have written wonderful books on Creation Science. These show numerous scientific proofs that the earth can't be more than a few thousand years old and numerous scientific reasons why one life form cannot evolve into a completely new kind of life form.

There are also a few books on Creation History which show numerous historical documents from around the world confirming that all the nations originally recorded the true biblical knowledge of their origins.

The Bible records enough historical dates that we can know God created the earth and all life in it no earlier than about 4,000 BC. Therefore, life did not evolve and there is no such thing as macroevolution.

The following chart was adapted from *Ancient Post-Flood History*. The number under the date is simply the years from Creation. It details not only the dates from the Bible passages, but also the Jewish historical books of Jasher and the Seder Olam. All of these books give the same dates.

One can clearly see the number of years from Creation to the destruction of Solomon's Temple is exactly 3,338 years, no more or less. There are so many historical documents, that virtually all modern historians place the destruction of King Solomon's Temple at 586 or 587 BC.

Event	Bible	Jasher	Seder	Date
Adam created	Gen. 5:1	1:1	1	1
Seth born	Gen. 5:3	2:1	1	130
Enos born	Gen. 5:6	2:2	1	235
Cainan born	Gen. 5:9	2:10	1	325
Mahalaleel born	Gen. 5:12	2:15	1	395
Jared born	Gen. 5:15	2:37	1	460
Enoch born	Gen. 5:18	2:37	1	622
Methuselah born	Gen. 5:21	3:1	1	687
Lamech born	Gen. 5:25	3:13	1	874
Noah born	Gen. 5:28,29	4:1	1	1056
Flood occurred	Gen. 7:11	6:1	4	1656
Arphaxad born	Gen. 11:10	7:19	1	1658
Selah born	Gen. 11:12	7:19	1	1693
Eber born	Gen. 11:14	7:19	1	1723
Peleg born	Gen. 11:16	7:19	1	1757
Reu born	Gen. 11:18	7:22	1	1787
Serug born	Gen. 11:20	7:22	1	1819
Nahor born	Gen. 11:22	7:22	1	1849
Terah born	Gen. 11:24	7:22	1	1878
Abraham born	Gen. 11:26	8:51	1	1948
Abraham given prophecy	Gen. 15:13	13:17	1	2018
Isaac born	Gen. 21:5	21:1	1	2048
Jacob born	Gen. 25:26	26:16	3	2108
Joseph born	Gen. 30:24	31:21	2	2199
Joseph enslaved	Gen. 37:2	41:9	2	2216
Joseph vice-Pharaoh	Gen. 41:46	49:38	2	2228
Seven-year famine began	Gen. 41:54	50:19		2237
Jacob migrated to Egypt	Gen. 47:28	55:26	2	2238
Jacob died	Gen. 47:28	56:1	2	2255
Joseph died	Gen. 50:26	59:25		2309
Exodus	Ex. 12:41	81:3	3	2448
Moses died	Deut. 31:1-2	87:10	10	2488
Joshua died	Jos. 24:29	90:47	11	2516
Temple Dedication	1 King. 6:1,38		15	2935
Temple Destruction			28	3338

The following websites provide information on the young age of the earth from a scientific and histoical perspectives.

· Institute of Creation Research
    www.icr.org

Answers in Genesis
    www.answersingenesis.org

Creation History
    www.creationhistory.us

Recently Fulfilled Prophecies

The third point of the Three-Fold Witness is to have a premillennial view of prophecies, both literal and typological, and especially the ones fulfilled in our life time because they are the most helpful in leading people to the Lord.

The following is a chart from the book *Ancient Prophecies Revealed*. It lists fifty plus prophecies that have been fulfilled since Israel became a nation in AD 1948. These, plus the next fifteen yet-to-be fulfilled prophecies, are given for your information. For a detailed description of these and many others, see *Ancient Prophecies Revealed*.

Date	Prophecy	References
1948	1. Israel will be reestablished as a nation	Isa. 11:11
	2. British ships will be the first to bring the Jewish people home	Isa. 60:9
	3. Israel will come back as one nation, not two	Hosea 1:11; Ezek. 37:18 ,19,22
	4. The nation of Israel will be born in a day	Isa. 66:8
	5. Israel will be reestablished with a leader named David	Hosea 3:5
	6. The revived state will be named "Israel"	Ezek. 37:11
	7. The Star of David will be on the Israeli flag	Isa. 11:10
	8. The nation will be reestablished in the ancient land of Canaan	Jer. 30:2,3; Ezek. 37:12
	9. Israel will no longer speak of being freed from Egypt	Jer. 16:14,15
	10. Israel will not be restored as a monarchy	Mic. 5:5
	11. Israel will be established on the date predicted	Dan 4; Ezek. 4:4-6
	12. The Hebrew language will be revived in Israel	Jer. 31:23
	13. Jerusalem will be initially divided	Zech. 14:1-3
	14. Jordan will occupy the West Bank	Zeph. 2:8; Zech. 12:1-7
	15. Israel will be initially restored without Jerusalem	Zech. 12:1-7
	16. Israel will have a fierce military (firepot)	Zech. 12:1-7; Isa. 41

	17. Dead Sea Scrolls will be found	Isa. 29:1-4
	18. Israel will be reestablished by the fourth craftsman	Zech 1:18-21
	19. The Jewish people will come back in unbelief	Ezek. 37:7-8,11
	20. First Shepherd will arise	Mic. 5:5-8
1949	21. Yemenite Jews will return	Isa. 43:3-7
1951	22. Israel will control Ashkelon	Zech. 9:1-8
1953	23. Egypt will no longer have kings (Suez crises)	Zech. 10:9-11
1967	24. Second Shepherd will arise	Mic. 5:5-8
	25. The 1967 war will occur on the date predicted	Dan. 5
	26. Five Egyptian cities will be conquered by the Israelis	Isa. 19:16-18
	27. Jordan will give up the West Bank	Zech. 12:6
	28. West Bank Jews will go home to Jerusalem	Zech. 12:6
1968	29. Israel will control Ashdod	Zech. 9:1-8
1973	30. Yom Kippur War will occur	Mic. 5:5-8
	31. Jerusalem will be a burden to all nations	Zech. 12:2,3
1980	32. The shekel will be revived as Israeli currency	Ezek. 45:1,2
1981	33. Third Shepherd will arise	Mic. 5:5-8
	34. Israel will attack Iraqi (nuclear) facility	Mic. 5:5-8
1982	35. Israel will give back the Sinai Peninsula	Zech. 10:6
	36. First Lebanese War will occur (firepot)	Zech. 12:6
1989	37. The Berlin Wall will fall	Ezek. 38:4-6
1990	38. Ethiopian Jews will be brought to Israel	Isa. 18:1-7
~2000	39. Cities will be restored and Israel will have non-Jewish farmers	Isa. 61:4,5; Zeph. 2
	40. Jerusalem will grow beyond its old walls	Zech. 2:4,5
	41. Land of Israel will be divided by its rivers and by Muslims	Isa. 18:1-7
	42. Tourists will fly in and support Israel	Isa. 60:8-10; Isa. 61
	43. There will be constant planting and reaping (crops)	Amos 9:13-15
	44. Forests will reappear in Israel (cedar, etc)	Isa. 41:18-20
	45. Desolate land and cities will be restored	Ezek. 36:33-36
	46. Five cities will stay desolate	Matt. 11:20-24
	47. Muslims will not "reckon Israel among nations"	Num. 23:9
	48. Israel will inherit remnant of Edom /Palestinians	Amos 9:12
	49. Satellite-television communication systems invented	Rev. 17:8
2004	50. Sanhedrin will be reestablished	Matt. 24:15,20

89

Epistle of Barnabas

2005	51. Palestinians will want Jerusalem as their capital	Ezek. 36:2,7,10-11
	52. Gaza will be forsaken	Zeph. 2:4
	53. Russia and Iran will sign a military defense pact	Ezek. 38:3-8
2006	54. Second Lebanese War will occur	Psalm 83:1-18

The fifteen prophecies scheduled to occur after 2008 are given below.

Date	Prophecy	References
2008		
	55. An independent state will be created out of the West Bank	Dan. 11:45
	56. Fourth Shepherd's Syrian war will occur	Mic. 5:1-8
	57. Fifth Shepherd's Syrian war will occur	Mic. 5:1-8
	58. Lebanon-Jordan war will occur	Zech. 10-11; Obad. 1:19
	59. Sephardic Jews will return to Israel, & populate the Negev	Obad. 1:20
	60. Sixth Shepherd's Syrian war will occur	Mic. 5:1-8
	61. Damascus will be destroyed	Isa. 17:1
	62. Gog-Magog War will occur immediately after Israel wins another war	Ezek. 38
	63. Rise of the ten nations occurs after the Gog-Magog War	Dan. 8,11
	64. Increased understanding of prophecies will occur	Dan. 12:4
	65. Children will be rebellious and society will be materialistic	Mark 13:12; 1 Tim. 3:23
	66. Jesus' words will never be forgotten	Mat. 24:15
	67. Christians will be hated for Jesus' Name's sake	Luke 21:17
	68. The apostasy of the church will fully form	
	69. The Rapture of the believing church will occur	
	70. The seven-year Tribulation will begin	

See the section on the apostasy of the church and the Rapture in *Ancient Prophecies Revealed* for full details.

Appendix A,
Greek Text of The Epistle of Barnabas

Chapter 1

Χαιρετε, υιοι και θυγατερες, εν ονοματι κυριου του αγαπησαντος ημας, εν ειρηνη.

μεγαλων μεν οντων και πλουσιων των του θεου δικαιωματων εις υμας, υπερ τι και καθ υπερβολην υπερευφραινομαι επι τοις μακαριοις και ενδοξοις υμων πνευμασιν· ουτως εμφυτον της δωρεας πνευματικης χαριν ειληφατε.

διο και μαλλον συγχαιρω εμαυτω ελπιζων σωθηναι, οτι αληθως βλεπω εν υμιν εκκεχυμενον απο του πλουσιου της πηγης κυριου πνευμα εφ υμας. ουτω με εξεπληξεν επι υμων η επιποθητη οψις υμων.

πεπεισμενος ουν τουτο και συνειδως εμαυτω, οτι εν υμιν λαλησας πολλα επισταμαι, οτι εμοι συνωδευσεν εν οδω δικαιοσυνης κυριος, και παντως αναγκαζομαι καγω εις τουτο, αγαπαν υμας υπερ την ψυχην μου, οτι μεγαλη πιστις και αγαθη εγκατοικει εν υμιν ελπιδι ζωης αυτου.

λογισαμενος ουν τουτο, οτι εαν μεληση μοι περι υμων του μερος τι μεταδουναι αφ ου ελαβον, οτι εσται μοι τοιουτοις πνευμασιν υπηρετησαντι εις μισθον, εσπουδασα κατα μικρον υμιν πεμπειν, ινα μετα της πιστεως υμων τελειαν εχητε την γνωσιν.

Τρια ουν δογματα εστιν κυριου· ζωης ελπις, αρχη και τελος πιστεως ημων, και δικαιοσυνη, κρισεως αρχη και τελος, αγαπε ευφροσυνης και αγαλλιασεως, εργων εν δικαιοσυνη μαρτυρια.

εγνωρισεν γαρ ημιν ο δεσποτης δια των προφητων τα παρεληλυθοτα και τα ενεστωτα, και των μελλοντων δους απαρχας ημιν γευσεως. ων τα καθ εκαστα βλεποντες

ενεργουμενα, καθως ελαλησεν, οφειλομεν πλουσιωτερον
και υψηλοτερον προσαγειν τω φοβω αυτου.
εγω δε, ουχ ως διδασκαλος αλλ ως εις εξ υμων, υποδειξω
ολιγα δι ων εν τοις παρουσιν ευφρανθησεσθε.

Chapter 2

Ημερων ουν ουσων πονηρων και αυτου του ενεργουντος
εχοντος την εξουσιαν, οφειλομεν εαυτοις προσεχοντες
εκζητειν τα δικαιωματα κυριου.
της ουν πιστεως ημων εισιν βοηθοι φοβος και υπομονη,
τα δε συνμαχουντα ημιν μακροθυμια και εγκρατεια.
τουτων μενοντων τα προς κυριον αγνως,
συνευφραινονται αυτοις σοφια, συνεσις, επιστημη,
γνωσις.
πεφανερωκεν γαρ ημιν δια παντων των προφητων οτι
ουτε θυσιων ουτε ολοκαυτωματων ουτε προσφορων
χρηζει, λεγων οτε μεν·
Τι μοι πληθος των θυσιων υμων; λεγει κυριος. πληρης
ειμι ολοκαυτωματων, και στεαρ αρνων και αιμα ταυρων
και τραγων ου βουλομαι, ουδ αν ερχησθε οφθηναι μοι. τις
γαρ εξεζητησεν ταυτα εκ των χειρων υμων· πατειν μου
την αυλην ου προσθησεσθε. εαν φερηε σεμιδαλιν,
ματαιον· θυμιαμα βδελυγμα μοι εστιν· τας νεομηνιας
υμων και τα σαββατα ουκ ανεχομαι.
ταυτα ουν κατηργησεν, ινα ο καινος νομος του κυριου
ημων Ιησου Χριστου, ανευ ζυγου αναγκης ων, μη
ανθρωποποιητον εχη την προσφοραν.
λεγει δε παλιν προς αυτους· Μη εγω ενετειλαμην τοις
πατρασιν υμων εκπορευομενοις εκ γης Αιγυπτου,
προσενεγκαι μοι ολοκαυτωματα και θυσιας;
αλλ η τουτο ενετειλαμην αυτοις· Εκαστος υμων κατα του
πλησιον εν τη καρδια αυτου κακιαν μη μνησικακειτω, και
ορκον ψευδη μη αγαπατε.

αισθανεσθαι ουν οφειλομεν, μη οντες ασυνετοι, την γνωμην της αγαθωσυνης του πατρος ημων, οτι ημιν λεγει, θελων ημας μη ομοιως πλανωμενους εκεινοις ζητειν πως προσαγωμεν αυτω.

ημιν ουν ουτως λεγει· Θυσια τω θεω καρδια συντετριμμενη, οσμη ευωδιας τω κυριω καρδια δοξαζουσα τον πεπλακοτα αυτην. ακριβευεσθαι ουν οφειλομεν, αδελφοι, περι της σωτηριας ημων, ινα μη ο πονηρος παρεισδυσιν πλανης ποιησας εν ημιν εκσφενδονηση ημας απο της ζωης ημων.

Chapter 3

Λεγει ουν παλιν περι τουτων προς αυτους· Ινα τι μοι νηστευετε, λεγει κυριος, ως σημερον ακουσθηναι εν κραυγη την φωνην υμων; ου ταυτην την νηστειαν εξελεξαμην, λεγει κυριος, ουκ ανθρωπον ταπεινουντα την ψυχην αυτου·

ουδ αν καμψητε ως κρικον τον τραχηλον υμων και σακκον ενδυσησθε και σποδον υποστρωσητε, ουδ ουτως καλεσετε νηστειαν δεκτην.

προς ημας δε λεγει· Ιδου αυτη η νηστεια ην εγω εξελεξαμην, λεγει κυριος· λυε παν συνδεσμον αδικιας, διαλυε στραγγαλιας βιαιων συναλλαγματων, αποστελλε τεθραυσμενους εν αφεσει, και πασαν αδικον συγγραφην διασπα. διαθρυπτε πεινωσιν τον αρτον σου, και γυμνον εαν ιδης περιβαλε· αστεγους εισαγε εις τον οικον σου, και εαν ιδης ταπεινον, ουχ υπεροψη αυτον, ουδε απο των οικειων του σπερματος σου.

τοτε ραγησεται πρωιμον το φως σου, και τα ιαματα σου ταχεως ανατελει, και προπορευσεται εμπροσθεν σου η δικαιοσυνη, και η δοξα του θεου περιστελει σε.

τοτε βοησεις, και ο θεος επακουσεται σου, ει λαλουντος σου ερει· Ιδου, παρειμι, εαν αφελης απο σου συνδεσμον και χειροτονιαν και ρημα γογγυσμου, και δως πεινωντι τον αρτον σου εκ ψυχης σου, και ψυχην τεταπεινωμενην ελεησησ.

εις τουτο ουν, αδελφοι, ο μακροθυμος προβλεψας, ως εν ακεραιοσυνη πιστευσει ο λαος ον ητοιμασεν εν τω ηγαπημενω αυτου, προεφανερωσεν ημιν περι παντων, ινα μη προσρησσωμεθα ως επηλυτοι τω εκεινων νομω.

Chapter 4

Δει ουν ημας περι των ενεστωτων επιπολυ εραυνωντας εκζητειν τα δυναμενα ημας σωζειν. φυγωμεν ουν τελειως απο παντων των εργων της ανομιας, μηποτε καταλαβη ημας τα εργα της ανομιας· και μισησωμεν την πλανην του νυν καιρου, ινα εις τον μελλοντα αγαπηθωμεν.

μη δωμεν τη εαυτων ψυχη ανεσιν, ωστε εχειν αυτην εξουσιαν μετα αμαρτωλων και πονηρων συντρεχειν, μηποτε ομοιωθωμεν αυτοις.

το τελειον σκανδαλον ηγγικεν, περι ου γεγραπται, ως Ενωχ λεγει. εις τουτο γαρ ο δεσποτης συντετμηκεν τους καιρους και τας ημερας, ινα ταχυνη ο ηγαπημενος αυτου και επι την κληρονομιαν ηξη.

λεγει δε ουτως και ο προφητης· βασιλειαι δεκα επι της γης βασιλευσουσιν, και εξαναστησεται οπισθεν αυτων μικρος βασιλευς, ος ταπειςωσει τρεις υφ εν των βασιλειων

ομοιως περι του αυτου λεγει Δανιηλ· Και ειδον το τεταρτον θηριον πονηρον και ισχυρον και χαλεπωτερον παρα παντα τα θηρια της γης, και ως εξ αυτου ανετειλεν δεκα κερατα, και εξ αυτων μικρον κερας παραφυαδιον, και ως εταπεινωσεν υφ εν τρια των μεγαλων κερατων.

συνιεναι ουν οφειλετε. ετι δε και τουτο ερωτω υμας ως εις εξ υμων ων, ιδιως δε και παντας αγαπων υπερ την ψυχην μου, προσεχειν νυν εαυτοις και μη ομοιουσθαι τισιν, επισωρευοντας ταις αμαρτιαις υμων λεγοντας οτι η διαθηκη {υμων υμιν μενει. ημων μεν·} αλλ εκεινοι ουτως εις τελος απωλεσαν αυτην, λαβοντος ηδη του Μωυσεως. λεγει γαρ η γραφη· Και ην Μωυσης εν τω ορει νηστευων ημερας τεσσαρακοντα και νυκτας τεσσαρακοντα και ελαβεν την διαθηκην απο του κυριου, πλακας λιθινας γεγραμμενας τω δακτυλω της χειρος του κυριου.

αλλα επιστραφεντες επι τα ειδωλα απωλεσαν αυτην. λεγει γαρ ουτως κυριος· Μωυση, Μωυση, καταβηθι το ταχος, οτι ηνομησεν ο λαος σου, ους εξηγαγες εκ γης Αιγυπτου. και συνηκεν Μωυσης και εριψεν τας δυο πλακας εκ των χειρων αυτου, και συνετριβη αυτων η διαθηκη, ινα η του ηγαπημενου Ιησου ενκατασφραγισθη εις την καρδιαν ημων εν ελπιδι της πιστεως αυτου.

πολλα δε θελων γραφειν, ουχ ως διδασκαλος αλλ ως πρεπει αγαπωντι αφ ων εχομεν μη ελλειπειν, γραφειν εσπουδασα, περιψημα υμων. Διο προσεχωμεν εν ταις εσχαταις ημεραις, ουδεν γαρ ωφελησει ημας ο πας χρονος της πιστεως ημων, εαν μη νυν εν τω ανομω καιρω και τοις μελλουσιν σκανδαλοις, ως πρεπει υιοις θεου, αντιστωμεν, ινα μη σχη παρεισδυσιν ο μελας

φυγωμεν απο πασης ματαιοτητος, μισησωμεν τελειως τα εργα της πονηρας οδου. μη καθ εαυτους ενδυνοντες μοναζετε ως ηδη δεδικαιωμενοι, αλλ επι το αυτο συνερχομενοι συνζητειτε περι του κοινη συμφεροντος.

λεγει γαρ η γραφη· ουαι οι συνετοι εαυτοις και ενωπιον εαυτων επιστημονες. γενωμεθα πνευματικοι, γενωμεθα ναος τελειος τω θεω. εφ οσον εστιν εν ημιν, μελετωμεν τον φοβον του θεου και φυλασσειν αγωνιζωμεθα τας εντολας αυτου, ινα εν τοις δικαιωμασιν αυτου ευφρανθωμεν.

ο κυριος απροσωπολημπτως κρινει τον κοσμον. εκαστος καθως εποιησεν κομιειται· εαν η αγαθος, η δικαιοσυνη αυτου προηγησεται αυτου· εαν η πονηρος, ο μισθος της πονηριας εμπροσθεν αυτου·

ινα μηποτε επαναπαυομενοι ως κλητοι επικαθυπνωσωμεν ταις αμαρτιαις ημων, και ο πονηρος αρχων λαβων την καθ ημων εξουσιαν απωσηται ημας απο της βασιλειας του κυριου.

ετι δε κακεινο, αδελφοι μου, νοειτε· οταν βλεπετε μετα τηλικαυτα σημεια και τερατα γεγονοτα εν τω Ισραηλ, και ουτως ενκαταλελειφθαι αυτους, προσεχωμεν, μηποτε, ως γεγραπται, πολλοι κλητοι, ολιγοι δε εκλεκτοι ευρεθωμεν.

Chapter 5

Εις τουτο γαρ υπεμεινεν ο κυριος παραδουναι την σαρκα εις καταφθοραν, ινα τη αφεσει των αμαρτιων αγνισθωμεν, ο εστιν εν τω αιματι του ραντισματος αυτου.

γεγραπται γαρ περι αυτου α μεν προς τον Ισραηλ, α δε προς ημας· λεγει δε ουτως· Ετραυματισθη δια τας ανομιας ημων και μεμαλακισται δια τας αμαρτιας ημων· τω μωλωπι αυτου ημεις ιαθημεν. ως προβατον επι σφαγην ηχθη και ως αμνος αφωνος εναντιον του κειραντος αυτον.

ουκουν υπερευχαριστειν οφειλομεν τω κυριω, οτι και τα παρεληλυθοτα ημιν εγνωρισεν και εν τοις ενεστωσιν ημας εσοφισεν, και εις τα μελλοντα ουκ εσμεν ασυνετοι.

λεγει δε η γραφη· Ουκ αδικως εκτεινεται δικτυα πτερωτοις. τουτο λεγει οτι δικαιως απολειται ανθρωπος, ος εχων οδου δικαιοσυνης γνωσιν, εαυτον εις οδον σκοτους αποσυνεχει.

ετι δε και τουτο, αδελφοι μου· ει ο κυριος υπεμεινεν παθειν περι της ψυχης ημων, ων παντος του κοσμου κυριος, ω ειπεν ο θεος απο καταβολης κοσμου· Ποιησωμεν ανθρωπον κατ εικονα και καθ ομοιωσιν ημετεραν, πως ουν υπεμεινεν υπο χειρος ανθρωπων παθειν; μαθετε.

οι προφηται, απ αυτου εχοντες την χαριν, εις αυτον εμπροφητευσαν. αυτος δε ινα καταργηση τον θανατον και την εκ νεκρων αναστασιν δειξη, οτι εν σαρκι εδει αυτον φανερωθηναι, υπεμεινεν,

ινα και τοις πατρασιν την επαγγελιαν αποδω και, αυτος
εαυτω τον λαον τον καινον ετοιμαζων, επιδειξη, επι της
γης ων, οτι την αναστασιν αυτος ποιησας κρινει.

περας γε τοι διδασκων τον Ισραηλ και τηλικαυτα τερατα
και σημεια ποιων, εκηρυσσεν και υπερηγαπησεν αυτον.

οτε δε τους ιδιους αποστολους τους μελλοντας κηρυσσειν
το ευαγγελιον αυτου εξελεξατο, οντας υπερ πασαν
αμαρτιαν ανομωτερους ινα δειξη οτι ουκ ηλθεν καλεσαι
δικαιους αλλα αμαρτωλους, τοτι εφανερωσεν εαυτον
ειναι υιον θεου.

ει γαρ μη ηλθεν εν σαρκι, ουδ αν πως οι ανθρωποι
εσωθησαν βλεποντες αυτον· οτε τον μελλοντα μη ειναι
ηλιον, εργον των χειρων αυτου υπαρχοντα, εμβλεποντες
ουκ ισχυουσιν εις τας ακτινας αυτου αντοφθαλμησαι.

ουκουν ο υιος του θεου εις τουτο εν σαρκι ηλθεν, ινα το
τελειον των αμαρτιων ανακεφαλαιωση τοις διωξασιν εν
θανατω τους προφητας αυτου.

ουκουν εις τουτο υπεμεινεν. λεγει γαρ ο θεος την πληγην
της σαρκος αυτου οτι εξ αυτων· Οταν παταξωσιν τον
ποιμενα εαυτων, τοτε απολειται τα προβατα της ποιμενης.

αυτος δε ηθελησεν ουτω παθειν, εδει γαρ ινα επι ξυλου
παθη. λεγει γαρ ο προφητευων επ αυτω· Φεισαι μου της
θυχης απο ρομφαιας, και· Καθηλωσον μου τας σαρκας,
οτι πονηρευομενων συναγωγαι επανεστησαν μοι.

και παλιν λεγει· Ιδου, τεθεικα μου τον νωτον εις
μαστιγας, τας δε σιαγονας μου εις ραπισματα, το δε
προσωπον μου εθηκα ως στερεαν πετραν.

Chapter 6

Οτε ουν εποιησεν την εντολην, τι λεγει; Τισ ο κρινομενος
μοι; αντιστητω μοι· η τις ο δικαιουμενος μοι; εγγισατω
τω παιδι κυριου.

ουαι υμιν, οτι υμεις παντες ως ιματιον παλαιωθησεσθε,
και σης καταφαγεται υμας. και παλιν λεγει προφητης,

επει ως λιθος ισχυρος ετεθη εις συντριβην· Ιδου, εμβαλω εις τα θεμελια Σιων λιθον πολυτελη, εκλεκτον, ακρογωνιαιον, εντιμον.

ειτα τι λεγει; Και ος ελπισει επ αυτον ζησεται εις τον αιωνα. επι λιθον ουν ημων η ελπις; μη γενοιτο· αλλ επει εν ισχυι τεθεικεν την σαρκα αυτου ο κυριος. λεγει γαρ· Και εθηκεν με ως στερεαν πετραν.

λεγει δε παλιν ο προφητης· Λιθον ον απεδοκιμασαν οι οικοδομουντες, ουτος εγενηθη εις κεφαλην γωνιας. και παλιν λεγει· Αυτη εστιν η ημερα η μεγαλη και θαυμαστη, ην εποιησεν ο κυριος.

απλουστερον υμιν γραφω, ινα συνιητε, εγω περιψημα της αγαπης υμων.

τι ουν λεγει παλιν ο προφητης; Περιεσχεν με συναγωγη πονηρευομενων, εκυκλωσαν με ωσει μελισσαι κηριον, και· Επι τον ιματισμον μου εβαλον κληρον.

εν σαρκι ουν αυτου μελλοντος φανερουσθαι και πασχειν, προεφανερωθη το παθος. λεγει γαρ ο προφητης επι τον Ισραηλ· Ουαι τη ψυχη αυτων, οτι βεβουλευνται βουλην πονηραν καθ εαυτων, ειποντες· Δησωμεν τον δικαιον, οτι δυσχρηστος ημιν εστιν.

τι λεγει ο αλλος προφητης Μωυσης αυτοις; Ιδου, ταδε λεγει κυριος ο θεος· Εισελθατε εις την γην αγαθην, ην ωμοσεν κυριος τω Αβρααμ και Ισαακ και Ιακωβ, και κατακληρονομησατε αυτην, γην ρεουσαν γαλα και μελι.

τι δε λεγει η γνωσις, μαθετε· Ελπισατε επι τον εν σαρκι μελλοντα φανερουσθαι υμιν Ιησουν. ανθρωπος γαρ γη εστιν πασχουσα· απο προσωπου γαρ της γης η πλασις του Αδαμ εγενετο.

τι ουν λεγει· Εις την γην την αγαθην, γην ρεουσαν γαλα και μελι; ευλογητος ο κυριος ημων, αδελφοι, ο σοφιαν και νουν θεμενος εν ημιν των κρυφιων αυτου. λεγει γαρ ο προφητης παραβολην κυριου· τις νοησει, ει μη σοφος και επιστημων και αγαθων τον κυριον αυτου;

επει ουν ανακαινισας ημας εν τη αφεσει των αμαρτιων, εποιησεν ημας αλλον τυπον, ως παιδιων εχειν την ψυχην, ως αν δη αναπλασσοντος αυτου ημας.

λεγει γαρ η γραφη περι ημων, ως λεγει τω υιω· Ποιησωμεν κατ εικονα και καθ ομοιωσιν ημων τον ανθρωπον, και αρχετωσαν των θηριων της γης και των πετεινων του ουρανου και των ιχθυων της θαλασσης. και ειπεν κυριος, ιδων το καλον πλασμα ημων· Αυξανεσθε και πληθυνεσθε και πληρωσατε την γην. ταυτα προς τον υιον.

παλιν σοι επιδειξω πως προς ημας λεγει κυριος. δευτεραν πλασιν επ εσχατων εποιησεν. λεγει δε κυριος· Ιδου, ποιω τα εσχατα ως τα πρωτα. εις τουτο ουν εκηρυξεν ο προφητης· Εισελθατε εις γην ρεουσαν γαλα και μελι, και κατακυριευσατε αυτης.

ιδε ουν ημεις αναπεπλασμεθα, καθως παλιν εν ετερω προφητη λεγει· Ιδου, λεγει κυριος, εξελω τουτων, τουτεστιν ων προεβλεπεν το πνευμα κυριου, τας λιθινας καρδιας, και εμβαλω σακινας, οτιν αυτος εν σαρκι εμελλεν φανερουσθαι και εν ημιν κατοικειν.

ναος γαρ αγιος, αδελφοι μου, τω κυριω το κατοικητηριον ημων της καρδιας.

λεγει γαρ κυριος παλιν· Και εν τινι οφθησομαι τω κυριω τω θεω μου και δοξασθησομαι; εξομολογησομαι σοι εν εκκλησια αδελφων μου, και ψαλω σοι αναμεσον εκκλησιας αγιων. ουκουν ημεις εσμεν ους εισηγαγεν εις την γην την αγαθην.

τι ουν το γαλα και το μελι; οτι πρωτον το παιδιον μελιτι, ειτα γαλακτι ζωοποιειται. ουτως ουν και ημεις τη πιστει της επαγγελιας και τω λογω ζωοποιουμενοι ζησομεν κατακυριευοντες της γης.

προειρηκαμεν δε επανω· Και αυξανεσθωσαν και πληθυνεσθωσαν και αρχετωσαν των ιχθυων. τις ουν ο δυναμενος νυν αρχειν θηριων η ιχθυων η πετεινων του ουρανου; αισθανεσθαι γαρ οφειλομεν οτι το αρχειν εξουσιας εστιν, ινα τις επιταξας κυριευση.

ει ουν ου γινεται τουτο νυν, αρα ημιν ειρηκεν ποτε· οταν και αυτοι τελειωθωμεν κληρονομοι της διαθηκης κυριου γενεσθαι.

Chapter 7

Ουκουν νοειτε, τεκνα ευφροσυνης, οτι παντα ο καλος κυριος προεφανερωσεν ημιν, ινα γηωμεν ω κατα παντα ευχαριστουντες οφειλομεν αινειν.

ει ουν ο υιος του θεου, ων κυριος και μελλων κρινειν ζωντας και νεκρους, επαθεν ινα η πληγη αυτου ζωοποιηση ημας, πιστευσωμεν οτι ο υιος του θεου ουκ ηδυνατο παθειν ει μη δι ημας.

Αλλα και σταυρωθεις εποτιζετο οξει και χολη. ακουσατε πως περι τουτου πεφανερωκαν οι ιερεις του ναου· γεγραμμενης εντολης· Ος αν μη νηστευση την νηστειαν, θανατω εξολεθρευθησεται, ενετειλατο κυριος επει και αυτος υπερ των ημετερων αμαρτιων εμελλεν το σκευος του πνευματιος προσφερειν θυσιαν, ινα και ο τυπος ο γενομενος επι Ισαακ του προσενεχθεντος επι το θυσιαστηριον τελεσθη.

τι ουν λεγει εν τω προφητη; Και φαγετωσαν εκ του τραγου του προσφερομενου τη νηστεια υπερ πασων των αμαρτιων, προσεχετε ακριβως, και φαγετωσαν οι ιερεις μονοι παντες το εντερον απλυτον μετα οξους.

προς τι; επειδη εμε, υπερ αμαρτιων μελλοντα του λαου μου του καινου προσφερειν την σαρκα μου, μελλετε ποτιζειν χολην μετα οξους, φαγετε υμεις μονοι, του λαου νηστευοντος και κοπτομενου επι σακκου και σποδου, ινα δειξη οτι δει αυτον παθειν υπ αυτων.

α ενετειλατο προσεχετε· Λαβετε δυο τραγους καλους και ομοιους και προσενεγκατε, και λαβετω ο ιερευς τον ενα εις ολοκαυτωμα υπερ αμαρτιων.

τον δε ενα τι ποιησωσιν; επικαταρατος, φησιν, ο εις. προσεχετε πως ο τψπος του Ιησου φανερουται.

100

και εμπτυσατε παντες και κατακεντησατε και περιθετε το εριον το κοκκινον περι την κεφαλην αυτου, και ουτως εις ερημον βληθητω. και οταν γενηται ουτως, αγει ο βασταζων τον τραγον εις την ερημον, και αφαιρει το εριον και επιτιθησιν αυτο επι φρυγανον το λεγομενον ραχη{λ}, ου και τους βλαστους ειωθαμεν τρωγειν εν τη χωρα ευρισκοντες· ουτω μονης της ραχης οι καρποι γλυκεις εισιν.

τι ουν τουτο εστιν; προσεχετε· Τον μεν ενα επι το θυσιαστηριον, τον δε ενα επικαταρατον, και οτι τον επικαταρατον εστεφανωμενον. επειδη οψονται αυτον τοτε τη ημερα τον ποδηρη εχοντα τον κοκκινον περι την σαρκα και ερουσιν· Ουχ ουτος εστιν ον ποτε ημεις εσταυρωσαμεν και εξουθενησαμεν εμπτυσαντες; αληθως ουτος ην ο τοτε λεγων εαυτον υιον του θεου ειναι.

πως γαρ ομοιος εκεινω; εις τουτο ομοιους τους τραγους, καλους, ισους ινα οταν ιδωσιν αυτον τοτε ερχομενον, εκπλαγωσιν επι τη ομοιοτητι του τραγου. ουκουν ιδε τον τυπον του μελλοντος πασχειν Ιησου.

τι δε οτι το εριον εις μεσον των ακανθων τιθεασιν; τυπος εστιν του Ιησου τη εκκλησια θεμενος, οτι ος εαν θελη το εριον αραι το κοκκινον, δει αυτον πολλα παθειν δια το ειναι φοβεραν την ακανθαν, και θλιβεντα κυριευσαι αυτου. ουτω, φησιν, οι θελοντες με ιδειν και αψασθαι μου της βασιλειας οφειλουσιν θλιβεντες και παθοντες λαβειν με.

Chapter 8

Τινα δε δοκειτε τυπον ειναι, οτι εντεταλται τω Ισραηλ προσφερειν δαμαλιν τους ανδρας εν οις εισιν αμαρτιαι τελειαι, και σφαξαντας κατακαιειν, και αιρειν τοτε τα παιδια σποδον και βαλλειν εις αγγη, και περιτιθεναι το εριον το κοκκινον επι ξυλον, ιδε παλιν ο τυπος ο του σταυρου και το εριον το κοκκινον, και το υσσωπον, και ουτως ραντιζειν τα παιδια καθ ενα τον λαον, ινα αγνιζωνται απο των αμαρτιων;

νοειτε πως εν απλοτητι λεγεται υμιν· ο μοσχος ο Ιησους εστιν, οι προσφεροντες ανδρες αμαρτωλοι οι προσενεγκαντες αυτον επι την σπαγην. ειτα ουκετι ανδρες, ουκετι αμαρτωλων η δοξα.

οι ραντιζοντες παιδες οι ευαγγελισαμενοι ημιν την αφεσιν των αμαρτιων και τον αγνισμον της καρδιας, οις εδωκεν του ευαγγελιου την εξουσιαν, ουσιν δεκαδυο εις μαρτυριον των φυλων, οτι δεκαδυο φυλαι του Ισραηλ, εις το κηρυσσειν.

διατι δε τρεις παιδες οι ραντιζοντες; εις μαρτυριον Αβρααμ, Ισαακ, Ιακωβ, οτι ουτοι μεγαλοι τω θεω.

οτι δε το εριον επι το ξυλον· οτι η βασιλεια Ιησου επι ξυλου, και οτι οι ελπιζοντες επ αυτον ζησονται εις τον αιωνα.

διατι δε αμα το εριον και το υσσωπον; οτι εν τη βασιλεια αυτου ημεραι εσονται πονηραι και ρυπαραι, εν αις ημεις σωθησομεθα, οτι και ο αλγων σαρκα δια του ρυπου του υσσωπου ιαται.

και δια τουτο ουτως γενομενα ημιν μεν εστιν φανερα, εκεινοις δε σκοτεινα, οτι ουκ ηκουσαν φωνης κυριου.

Chapter 9

Λεγει γαρ παλιν περι των ωτιων, πως περιετεμεν ημων την καρδιαν. λεγει κυριος εν τω προφητη· Εις ακοην ωτιου υπηκουσαν μου. και παλιν λεγει· Ακοη ακουσονται οι πορρωθεν, α εποιησα γνωσονται, και· Περιτμηητε, λεγει κυριος, τας καρδιας υμων.

και παλιν λεγει· Ακουε, Ισραηλ, οτι ταδε λεγει κυριος οτ θεος σου. και παλιν το πνευμα κυριου προφητευει· Τις εστιν ο θελων ζησαι εις τον αιωνα; ακοη ακουσατω της φωνης του παιδος μου.

και παλιν λεγει· Ακουε, ουρανε, και ενωτιζου, γη, οτι
κυριος ελαλησεν ταυτα εις μαρτυριον. και παλιν λεγει·
Ακουσατε, τεκνα, φωνης βοωντος εν τη ερημω.
ουκουν περιετεμεν ημων τας ακοας, ινα ακουσαντες
λογον πιστευσωμεν ημεις. Αλλα και η περιτομη εφ η
πεποιθασιν κατηργηται, περιτομην γαρ ειρηκεν ου
σαρκος γενηθηναι. αλλα παρεβησαν, οτι αγγελος πονηρος
εσοφιζεν αυτους.
λεγει προς αυτους· Ταδε λεγει κυριος ο θεος υμων, ωδε
ευρισκω εντολην· Μη σπειρητε επ ακανθαις, περιτμηθητε
τω κυριω υμων. και τι λεγει; Περιτμηθητε την
σκληροκαρδιαν υμων, και τον τραχηλον υμων ου
σκληρυνειτε. λαβε παλιν· Ιδου, λεγει κυριος, παντα τα
εθνη απεριτμητα ακροβυστιαν, ο δε λαος ουτος
απεριτμητος καρδιας.
Αλλ ερεις· Και μην περιτετμηται ο λαος εις σφραγιδα.
αλλα και πας Συρος και Αραψ και παντες οι ιερεις των
ειδωλων· αρα ουν κακεινοι εκ της διαθηκης αυτων εισιν;
αλλα και οι Αιγυπτιοι εν περιτομη εισιν.
Μαθετε ουν, τεκνα αγαπης, περι παντων πλουσιως, οτι
Αβρααμ, πρωτος περιτομην δους, εν πνευματι προβλεψας
εις τον Ιησουν περιετεμεν, λαβων τριων γραμματων
δογματα.
λεγει γαρ· Και περιετεμεν Αβρααμ εκ του οικου αυτου
ανδρας δεκαοκτω και τρακοσιους. τις ουν η δοθεισα αυτω
γνωσισ; μαθετε οτι τους δεκαοκτω, Ι δεκα, Η οκτω· εχεις
Ιησουν. οτι δε ο σταυρος εν τω Τ ημελλεν εχειν την
χαριν, λεγει και τριακοσιους. δηλοι ουν τον μεν Ιησουν εν
τοις δυσιν γραμμασιν, και εν τω ενι τον σταυρον.
οιδεν ο την εμφυτον δωρεαν της διαθηκης αυτου θεμενος
εν ημιν. ουδεις γνησιωτερον εμαθεν απ εμου λογον, αλλα
οιδα οτι αξιοι εστε υμεις.

Epistle of Barnabas

Chapter 10

Οτι δε Μωυσης ειπεν· Ου φαγεσθε χοιρον ουτε αετον ουτε οξυπτερον ουτε κορακα, ουτε παντα ιχθυν ος ουκ εχει λεπιδα εν εαυτω, τρια ελαβεν εν τη συνεσει δογματα. περας γε τοι λεγει αυτοις εν τω Δευτερονομιω· Και διαθησομαι προς τον λαον τουτον τα κικαιωματα μου. αρα ουν ουκ εστιν εντολη θεου το μη τρωγειν, Μωυσης δε εν πνευματι ελαλησεν.

το ουν χοιριον προς τουτο ειπεν· ου κολληθηση, φησιν, ανθρωποις τοιουτοις, οιτινες εισιν ομοιοι χοιρων· τουτεστιν οταν σπαταλωσιν επιλανθανονται του κυριου, οταν δε υστερουνται, επιγινωσκουσιν τον κυριον, ως και ο χοιρος οταν τρωγει τον κυριον ουκ οιδεν, οταν δε πεινα κραυγαζει, και λαβων παλιν σιωπα.

Ουτε φαγη τον αετον ουδε τον εξυπτερον ουδε τον ικτινα ουδε τον κορακα· ου μη, φησιν, κολληθηση ουδε ομοιωθηση ανθρωποις τοιουτοις, οιτινες ουκ οιδασιν δια κοπου και ιδρωτος εαυτοις ποριζειν την τροφην, αλλα αρπαζουσιν τα αλλοτρια εν ανομια αυτων και επιτηρουσιν, εν ακεραιοσυνη περιπατουντες, και περιβλεπονται τινα εκδυσωσιν δια την πλεονεξιαν, ως και τα ορνεα ταυτα μονα εαυτοις ου ποριζει την τροφην, αλλα αργα καθημενα εκζητει πως αλλοτριας σαρκας φαγη, οντα λοιμα τη πονηρια αυτων.

Και ου φαγη, φησιν, σμυραιναν ουδε πωλυπα ουδε σηπιαν· ου μη φησιν, ομοιωθηση ανθρωποις τοιουτοις, οιτινες εις τελος εισιν ασεβεις και κεκριμενοι ηδη τω θανατω, ως και ταυτα τα ιχθυδια μονα επικαταρατα εν τω βυθω νηχεται, μη κολυμβωντα ως τα λοιπα, αλλα εν τη γη κατω του βυθου κατοικει.

αλλα και τον δασυποδα ου μη φαγη. προς τι; ου μη γενη, φησιν, παιδοφθορος ουδε ομοιωθηση τοις τοιουτοις, οτι ο λαγωος κατ ενιαυτον πλεονεκτει την αφοδευσιν· οσα γαρ ετη ζη, τοσαυτας εχει τρυπας.

Greek Text

αλλα ουδε την υαιναν φαγη· ου μη, φησιν, γενη μοιχος ουδε φθορευς ουδε ομοιωθηση τοις τοιουτοις. προς τι; οτιν το ζωον τουτο παρ ενιαυτον αλλασσει την φυσιν, και ποτε μεν αρρεν, ποτε δε θηλυ γινεται.
αλλα και την γαλην εμισησεν καλως. ου μη, φησιν, γενηθης τοιουτος, οιους ακουομεν ανομιαν ποιουντας εν τω στοματι δι ακαθαρσιαν, ουδε κολληθηση ταις ακαθαρτοις ταις την ανομιαν ποιουσαις εν τω στοματι. το γαρ ζωον τουτο τω στοματι κυει.
Περι μεν των βρωματων λαβων Μωυσης τρια δογματα ουτως εν πνευματι ελαλησεν, οι δε κατ επιθυμιαν της σαρκος ως περι βρωσεως προσεδεξαντο.
λαμβανει δε των αυτων τριων δογματων γνωσιν Δαυιδ, και λεγει· Μακαριος ανηρ ος ουκ επορευθη εν βουλη ασεβων, καθως και οι ιχθυες πορευονται εν σκοτει εις τα βαθη, και εν οδω αμαρτωλων ουκ εστη, καθως οι δοκουντες φοβεισθαι τον κυριον αμαρτανουσιν ως ο χοιρος, και επι καθεδραν λοιμων ουκ εκαθισεν, καθως τα πετεινα τα καθημενα εις αρπαγην. εχετε τελειως και περι της βρωσεως.
Παλιν λεγει Μωυσης· Φαγεσθε παν διχηλουν και μαρυκωμενον. τι λεγει; οτι την τροφην λαμβανων οιδεν τον τρεφοντα αυτον, και επ αυτω αναπαυομενος ευφραινεσθαι δοκει. καλως ειπεν βλεπων την εντολην. τι ουν λεγει; κολλασθε μετα των φοβουμενων τον κυριον, μετα των μελετωντων ο ελαβον διασταλμα ρηματος εν τη καρδια, μετα των λαλουντων τα δικαιωματα κυριου και τηρουντων, μετα των ειδοτων οτι η μελετη εστιν εργον ευφροσυνης και αναμαρυκωμενων τον λογον κυριου. τι δε το διχηλουν; οτι ο δικαιος και εν τουτω τω κοσμω περιπατει και τον αγιον αιωνα εκδεχεται. βλεπετε πως ενομοθετησεν Μωυσης καλως.
αλλα ποθεν εκεινοις ταυτα νοησαι η συνιεναι; ημεις δε δικαιως νοησαντες τας εντολας, λαλουμεν ως ηθελησεν ο κυριος. δια τουτο περιετεμεν τας ακοας ημων και τας καρδιας, ινα συνιωμεν ταυτα.

105

Chapter 11

Ζητησωμεν δε ει εμελησεν τω κυριω προφανερωσαι περι του υδατος και περι του σταυρου. περι μεν του υδατος, γεγραπται επι τον Ισραηλ πως το βαπτισμα το φερον αφεσιν αμαρτιων ου μη προσδεξονται, αλλ εαυτοις οικοδομησουσιν.

λεγει γαρ ο προφητης· Εκστηθι ουρανε, και επι τουτω πλειον φριξατω η γη, οτι δυο και πονηρα εοιησεν ο λαος ουτος· εμε εγκατελιπον, πηγην ζωης, και εαυτοις ωρυξαν βοθρον θανατου.

Μη πετρα ερημος εστιν το ορος το αγιον μου Σινα; εσεσθε γαρ ως πετεινου νοσσοι ανιπταμενοι νοσσιας αφηρημενοι.

και παλιν λεγει ο προφητης· Εγω πορευσομαι εμπροσθεν σου και ορη ομαλιω και πυλας χαλκας συντριψω και μοχλους σιδηρους συνκλασω, και δωσω σοι θησαυρος σκοτεινους, αποκρυφους, αορατους, ινα γνωσιν οτι εγω κυριος ο θεος, και· Κατοικησεις εν υψηλω σπηλαιω πετρας ισχυρας,

και· Το υδωρ αυτου πιστον· βασιλεα μετα δοξης οψεσθε, και η ψυχη υμων μελετησει φοβον κυριου.

και παλιν εν αλλω προφητη λεγει· Και εσται ο ταυτα ποιων ως το ξυλον το πεφυτευμενον παρα τας διεξοδους των υδατων, ο τον καρπον αυτου δωσει εν καιρω αυτου, και το φυλλον αυτου ουκ απορυησεται, και παντα οσα αν ποιη κατευοδωθησεται.

ουχ ουτως οι ασεβεις, ουχ ουτως, αλλ η ως ο χνους ον εκριπτει ο ανεμος απο προσωπου της γης. δια τουτο ουκ αναστησονται ασεβεις εν κρισει, ουδε αμαρτωλοι εν βουλη δικαιων, οτι γινωσκει κυριος οδον δικαιων, και οδος ασεβων απολειται.

αισθανεσθε πως το υδωρ και τον σταυρον επι το αυτο ωρισεν. τουτο γαρ λεγει μακαριοι οι επι τον σταυρον ελπισαντες κατεβησαν εις το υδωρ, οτι τον μεν μισθον λεγει εν καιρω αυτου· τοτε, φησιν, αποδωσω. νυν δε ο λεγει· Τα φυλλα ουκ απορυησεται. τουτο λεγει οτι παν ρημα ο εαν εξελευσεται εξ υμων δια του στοματος υμων εν πιστει και αγαπη εσται εις επιστροφην και ελπιδα πολλοις.

και παλιν ετερος προφητης λεγει· Και ην η γη του Ιακωβ επαινουμενη παρα πασαν την γην. τουτο λεγει· το σκευος του πνευματος αυτου δοξαζει.

ειτα τι λεγει; Και ην ποταμος ελκων εκ δεξιων, και ανεβαινεν εξ αυτου δενδρα ωραια· και ος αν φαγη εξ αυτων ζησεται εις τον αιωνα.

τουτο λεγει οτι ημεις μεν καταβαινομεν εις το υδωρ γεμοντες αμαρτιων και ρυπου, και αναβαινομεν καρποφορουντες εν τη καρδια, και τον φοβον και την ελπιδα εις τον Ιησουν εν τω πνευματι εχοντες. Και ος αν φαγη απο τουτων ζησεται εις τον αιωνα, τουτο λεγει· ος αν, φησιν, ακουση τουτων λαλουμενων και πιστευση ζησεται εις τον αιωνα.

Chapter 12

Ομοιως παλιν περι του σταυρου οριζει εν αλλω προφητη λεγοντι· Και τοτε ταυτα συντελεσθησεται; λεγει κυριος· Οταν ξυλον κλιθη και αναστη, και οταν εκ ξυλου αιμα σταξη. εχεις παλιν περι του σταυρου και του σταυρουσθαι μελλοντος.

λεγει δε παλιν τω Μωυση, πολεμουμενου του Ισραηλ υπο των αλλοφυλων, και ινα υπομνηση αυτους πολεμουμενους οτι δια τας αμαρτιας αυτων παρεδοθησαν εις θανατον, λεγει εις την καρδιαν Μωυσεως το πνευμα, ινα ποιηση τυπον σταυρου και του μελλοντος πασχειν, οτι εαν μη φησιν, ελπισωσιν επ αυτω, εις τον αιωνα πολεμηθησονται. τιθησιν ουν Μωυσης εν εφ εν οπλον εν μεσω της πυγμης, και σταθεις υψηλοτερος παντων

Epistle of Barnabas

εξετεινεν τας χειρας, και ουτως παλιν ενικα ο Ισραηλ. ειτα, οποταν καθειλεν, εθανατουντο.

προς τι; ινα γνωσιν οτι ου δυνανται σωθηναι εαν μη επ αυτω ελπισωσιν.

και παλιν εν ετερω προφητη λεγει· Ολην την ημεραν εξεπετασα τας χειρας μου προς λαον απειθη και αντιλεγοντα οδω δικαια μου.

παλιν Μωυσης ποιει τυπον του Ιησου, οτι δει αυτον παθειν, και αυτος ζωοποιησει ον δοξουσιν απολωλεκεναι εν σημειω, πιπτοντος του Ισραηλ. εποιησεν γαρ κυριος παντα οφιν δακνειν αυτους, και απεθνησκον, επειδη η παραβασις δια του οφεως εν Ευα εγενετο, ινα ελεγξη αυτους οτι δια την παραβασιν αυτων εις θλιψιν θανατου παραδοθησονται.

περας γε τοι αυτος Μωυσης εντειλαμενος· Ουκ εσται υμιν ουτε χωνευτον ουτε γλυπτον εις θεον υμιν, αυτος ποιει, ινα τυπον του Ιησου δειξη. ποιει ουν Μωυσης χαλκουν οφιν και τιθησιν ενδοξως, και κηρυγματι καλει τον λαον.

ελθοντες ουν επι το αυτο εδεοντο Μωυσεως ινα περι αυτων ανενεγκη δεησιν περι της ιασεως αυτων. ειπεν δε προς αυτους Μωυσης· Οταν, φησιν, δηχθη τις υμων, ελθετω επι τον οφιν τον επι του ξυλου επικειμενον και ελπισατω, πιστευσας οτι αυτος ων νεκρος δυναται ζωοποιησαι, και παραχρημα σωθησεται. και ουτως εποιουν. εχεις παλιν και εν τουτοις την δοξαν του Ιησου, οτι εν αυτω παντα και εις αυτον.

Τι λεγει παλιν Μωυσης Ιησου υιω Ναυη επιθεις αυτω τουτο το ονομα, οντι προφητη, ινα μονον ακουση πας ο λαος οτι ο πατηρ παντα φανεροι περι του υιου Ιησου;

λεγει ουν Μωυσης Ιησου υιω Ναυη επιθεις τουτο ονομα οποτε επεμψεν αυτον κατασκοπον της γης· Λαβε βιβλιον εις τας χειρας σου και γραψον α λεγει κυριος, οτι εκκοψει εκ ριζων τον οικον παντα του Αμαληκ ο υιος του θεου επ εσχατων των ημερων.

ιδε παλιν Ιησους, ουχι υιος ανθρωπου αλλα υιος του θεου, τυπω δε εν σαρκι φανερωθεις. Επει ουν μελλουσιν λεγειν οτι ο Χριστος υιος Δαυιδ εστιν, αυτος προφητευει Δαυιδ, φοβουμενος και συνιων την πλανην των αμαρτωλων· Ειπεν κυριος τω κυριω μου· Καθου εκ δεξιων μου εως αν θω τους εχθρους σου υποποδιον των ποδων σου.

και παλιν λεγει ουτως Ησαιας· Ειπεν κυριος τω Χριστω μου κυριω, ου εκρατησα της δεξιας αυτου, επακουσαι εμπροσθεν αυτου εθνη, και ισχυν βασιλεων διαρρηξω. ιδε πως Δαυιδ λεγει αυτον κυριον, και υιον ου λεγει.

Chapter 13

Ιδωμεν δε ει ουτος ο λαος κληρονομει η ο πρωτος, και η διαθηκη εις ημας η εις εκεινους.

ακουσατε ουν περι του λαου τι λεγει η γραφη· Εδειτο δε Ισαακ περι Ρεβεκκας της γυναικος αυτου, οτι στειρα ην· και συνελαβεν. ειτα εξηλθεν Ρεβεκκα πυθεσθαι παρα κυριου. και ειπεν κυριος προς αυτην· Δυο εθνη εν τη γαστρι σου και δυο λαοι εν τη κοιλια σου, και υπερεξει λαος λαου, και ο μειζων δουλευσει τω ελασσονι.

αισθανεσθαι οφειλετε τις ο Ισαακ και τις η Ρεβεκκα, και επι τινων δεδειχεν οτι μειζων ο λαος ουτος η εκεινος.

και εν αλλη προφητεια λεγει φανερωτερον ο Ιακωβ προς Ιωσηφ τον υιον αυτου, λεγων· Ιδου, ουκ εστερησεν με κυριος του προσωπου σου· προσαγαγε μοι τους υιους σου, ινα ευλογησω αυτους.

και προηγαγεν Εφραιμ και Μανασση, τον Μανασση θελων ινα ευλογηθη, οτι πρεσβυτερος ην· ο γαρ Ιωσηφ προσηγαγεν εις την δεξιαν χειρα του πατρος Ιακωβ. ειδεν δε Ιακωβ τυπον τω πνευματι του λαου του μεταξυ. και τι λεγει; Και εποιησεν Ιακωβ εναλλαξ τας χειρας αυτου και επεθηκεν την δεξιαν επι την κεφαλην Εφραιμ του δευτερου και νεωτερου, και ευλογησεν αυτον. και ειπεν Ιωσηφ προς Ιακωβ· Μεταθες σου την δεξιαν επι την κεφαλην Μανασση, οτι πρωτοτοκος μου υιος εστιν. και ειπεν Ιακωβ προς Ιωσηφ· Οιδα, τεκνον, οιδα· αλλ ο μειζων δουλευσει τω ελασσονι. και ουτος δε ευλογηθησεται.

βλεπετε επι τινων τεθεικεν τον λαον τουτον ειναι πρωτον, και της διαθηκες κληρονομον.

Ει ουν ετι και δια του Αβρααμ εμνησθη, απεχομεν το τελειον της γνωσεως ημων. τι ουν λεγει τω Αβρααμ, οτε μονος πιστευσας ετεθη εις δικαιοσυνην; Ιδου, τεθεικα σε, Αβρααμ, πατερα εθνων των πιστευοντων δι ακροβυστιας τω θεω.

Chapter 14

Ναι. αλλα ιδωμεν ει η διαθηκη ην ωμοσεν τοις πατρασιν δουναι τω λαω, ει δεδωκεν. δεδωκεν· αυτοι δε ουκ εγενοντο αξιοι λαβειν δια τας αμαρτιας αυτων.

λεγει γαρ ο προφητης· Και ην Μωυσης νηστευων εν ορει Σινα, του λαβειν την διαθηκην κυριου προς τον λαον, ημερας τεσσαρακοντα και νυκτας τεσσαρακοντα. και ελαβεν Μωυσης παρα κυριου τας δυο πλακας τας γεγραμμενας τω δακτυλω της χειρος κυριου εν πνευματι. και λαβων Μωυσης κατεφερεν προς τον λαον δουναι.

και ειπεν κυριος προς Μωυσην· Μωυση, Μωυση, καταβηθι το ταχος οτι ο λαος σου, ωον εξηγαγες εκ γης Αιγηπτου, ηνομησεν. και συνηκεν Μωυσης οτι εποιησαν εαυτοις παλιν χωνευματα, και εριψεν εκ των χειρων τας πλακας, και συνετριβησαν αι πλακες της διαθηκης κυριου.

Μωυσης μεν ελαβεν, αυτοι δε ουκ εγενοντο αξιοι. Πως δε ημεις ελαβομεν; μαθετε. Μωυσης θεραπων ων ελαβεν, αυτος δε ο κυριος ημιν εδωκεν εις λαον κληρονομιας, δι ημας υπομεινας.

εφανερωθη δε ινα κακεινοι τελειωθωσιν τοις αμαρτημασιν και ημεις δια του κληρονομουντος διαθηκην κυριου Ιησου λαβωμεν, ος εις τουτο ητοιμασθη, ινα αυτος φανεις τας ηδη δεδαπανημενας ημων καρδιας τω θανατω και παραδεδομενας τη της πλανης ανομια λυτρωσαμενος εκ του σκοτους, διαθηται εν ημιν διαθηκην λογω.

γεγραπται γαρ πως αυτω ο πατηρ εντελλεται, λυτρωσαμενον ημας εκ του σκοτους, ετοιμασαι εαυτω λαον αγιον.

λεγει ουν ο προφητης· Εγω κυριος ο θεος σου εκαλεσα σε εν δικαιοσυνη, και κρατησω της χειρος σου και ενισχυσω σε, και εδωκα σε εις διαθηκην γενους, εις φως εθνων, ανοιξαι οφθαλμους τυφλων, και εξαγαγειν εκ δεσμων πεπεδημενους και εξ οικου φυλακης καθημενους εν σκοτει. γινωσκομεν ουν ποθεν ελυτρωθημεν.

παλιν ο προφητης λεγει· Ιδου, τεθεικα σε εις φως εθνων, του ειναι σε εις σωτηριαν εως εσχατου της γης· ουτως λεγει κυριος ο λυτρωσαμενος σε θεος.

παλιν ο προφητης λεγει· Πνευμα κυριου επ εμε, ου εινεκεν με ευαγγελισασθαι ταπεινοις χαριν, απεσταλκεν με ιασασθαι τους συντετριμμενους την καρδιαν, κηρυξαι αιχμαλωτοις αφεσιν και τυφλοις αναβλεψιν, καλεσαι ενιαυτον κυριου δεκτον και ημεραν ανταποδοσεως, παρακαλεσαι παντας τους πενθουντας.

Chapter 15

Ετι ουν και περι του σαββατου γεγραπται εν τοις δεκα λογοις, εν οις ελαλησεν εν τω ορει Σινα προς Μωυσην κατα προσωπον· Και αγιασατε το σαββατον κυριου χερσιν καθαραις και καρδια καθαρα.

και εν ετερω λεγει· Εαν φυλαξωσιν οι υιοι μου το σαββατον, τοτε επιθησω το ελεος μου επ αυτους.

το σαββατον λεγει εν αρχη της κτισεως· Και εποιησεν ο θεος εν εξ ημεραις τα εργα των χειρων αυτου, και συνετελεσεν εν τη ημερα τη εβδομη και κατεπαυσεν εν αυτη, και ηγιασεν αυτην.

προσεχετε, τεκνα, τι λεγει το συνετελεσεν εν εξ ημεραις. τουτο λεγει, οτι εν εξακισχιλιοις ετεσιν συντελεσει κυριος τα συμπαντα, η γαρ ημερα παρ αυτω σημαινει χιλια ετη. αυτος δε μοι μαρτυρει λεγων· Ιδου, ημερα κυριου εσται ως χιλια ετη. ουκουν, τεκνα, εν εξ ημεραις, εν τοις εξακισχιλιοις ετεσιν, συντελεσθησεται τα συμπαντα.

Και κατεπαυσεν τη ημερα τη εβδομη. τουτο λεγει· οταν ελθων ο υιος αυτου καταργηση τον καιρον του ανομου και κρινει τους ασεβεις και αλλαξει τον ηλιον και την σεληνην και τους αστερας, τοτε καλως καταπαυσεται εν τη ημερα τη εβδομη.

περας γε τοι λεγει· Αγιασεις αυτην χερσιν καθαραις και καρδια καθαρα. ει ουν ην ο θεος ημεραν ηγιασεν, νυν τις δυναται αγιασαι καθαρος ων τη καρδια, εν πασιν πεπλανημεθα.

ει δε ου, αρα τοτε καλως καταπαυομενοι αγιασομεν αυτην οτε δυνησομεθα αυτοι δικαιωθεντες και απολαβοντες την επαγγελιαν, μηκετι ουσης της ανομιας, καινων δε γεγονοτων παντων υπο κυριου, τοτε δυνησομεθα αυτην αγιασαι, αυτοι αγιασθεντες πρωτον.

περας γε τοι λεγει αυτοις· Τας νεομηνιας υμων και τα σαββατα ουκ ανεχομαι. ορατε πως λεγει· ου τα νυν σαββατα εμοι δεκτα, αλλα ο πεποιηκα· εν ω καταπαυσας τα παντα αρχην ημερας ογδοης ποιησω, ο εστιν αλλου κοσμου αρχην.

διο και αγομεν την ημεραν την ογδοην εις ευφροσυνην, εν η και ο Ιησους ανεστη εκ νεκρων και φανερωθεις ανεβη εις ουρανους.

Chapter 16

Ετι δε και περι του ναου ερω υμιν, πως πλανωμενοι οι ταλαιπωροι εις την οικοδομην ηλπισαν, και ουκ επι τον θεον αυτων τον ποιησαντα αυτους, ως οντα οικον θεου. σχεδον γαρ ως τα εθνη αφιερωσαν αυτον εν τω ναω. αλλα πως λεγει κυριος καταργων αυτων; μαθετε· Τις εμετρησεν τον ουρανον σπιθαμη, η την γην δρακι; ουκ εγω, λεγει κυριος; ου ουρανος μοι θρονος, η δε γη υποποδιον των ποδων μου· ποιον οικον οικοδομησετε μοι, η τις τοπος της καταπαυσεως μου; εγνωκατε οτι ματαια η ελπις αυτων.
περας γε τοι παλιν λεγει· Ιδου, οι καθελοντες τον ναον τουτον, αυτοι αυτον οικοδομησουσιν.
γινεται. δια γαρ το πολεμειν αυτους καθηρεθη υπο των εχθρων, νυν και αυτοι οι των εχθρων υπηρεται ανοικοδομησουσιν αυτον.
παλιν ως εμελλεν η πολις και ο ναος και ο λαος Ισραηλ παραδιδοσθαι, εφανερωθη. λεγει γαρ η γραφη· Και εσται επ εσχατων των ημερων, και παραδωσει κυριος τα προβατα της νομης και την μανδραν και τον πυργον αυτων εις καταφθοραν. και εγενετο καθ α ελαλησεν κυριος.
Ζητησωμεν δε ει εστιν ναος θεου. εστιν, οπου αυτος λεγει ποιειν και καταρτιζειν. γεγραπται γαρ· Και εσται της εβδομαδος συντελουμενης, οικοδομηθησεται ναος θεου ενδοξως επι τω ονοματι κυριου.
ευρισκω ουν οτι εστιν ναος. πως ουν οικοδομηθησεται επι τω ονοματι κυριου; μαθετε· προ του ημας πιστευσαι τω θεω ην ημων το κατοικητηριον της καρδιας φθαρτον και ασθενες, ως αληθως οικοδομητος ναος δια χειρος, οτι ην πληρης μεν ειδωλολατρειας και ην οικος δαιμονιων, δια το ποιειν οσα ην εναντια τω θεω.
Οικοδομηθησεται δε επι τω ονοματι κυριου. προσεχετε δε, ινα ο ναος του κυριου ενδοξως οικοδομηθη. πως; μαθετε· λαβοντες την αφεσιν των αμαρτιων και

ελπισαντες επι το ονομα εγενομεθα καινοι, παλιν εξ αρχης κτιζομενοι· διο εν τω κατοικητηριω ημων αληθως ο θεος κατοικει.

πως; ο λογος αυτου της πιστεως, η κλησις αυτου της επαγγελιας, η σοφια των δικαιωματων, αι εντολαι της διδαχης, αυτος εν ημιν προφητευων, αυτος εν ημιν κατοικων, τοις τω θανατω δεδουλωμενοις ανοιγων ημιν την θυραν του ναου, ο εστιν στομα, μετανοιαν διδους ημιν εισαγει εις τον αφθαρτον ναον.

ο γαρ ποθων σωθηναι βλεπει ουκ εις τον ανθρωπον αλλ εις τον εν αυτω κατοικουντα και λαλουντα, επ αυτω εκπλησσομενος επι τω μηδεποτε μητε αυτος ποτε επιτεθυμηκεναι ακουειν. τουτο εστιν πνευματικος ναος οικοδομουμενος τω κυριω.

Chapter 17

Εφ οσον ην εν δυνατω και απλοτητι δηλωσαι υμιν, ελπιζει μου η ψυχη {τη επιθυμια μου} μη παραλελοιπεναι τι {των ανηκοντων εις σωτεριαν}.

εαν γαρ περι των ενεστωτων η μελλοντων γραφω υμιν, ου μη νοησητε δια το εν παραβολαις κεισθαι. ταυτα μεν ουτως.

Chapter 18

Μεταβωμεν δε και επι ετεραν γνωσιν και διδαχην. οδοι δυο εισιν διδαχης και εξουσιας, η τε του φωτος και η του σκοτους· διαφορα δε πολλη των δυο οδων. εφ ης μεν γαρ εισιν τεταγμενοι φωταγωγοι αγγελοι του θεου, εφ ης δε αγγελοι του Σατανα.

και ο μεν εστιν κυριος απο αιωνων και εις τους αιωνας, ο δε αρχων καιρου του νυν της ανομιας.

114

Chapter 19

Η ουν οδος του φωτος εστιν αυτη· εαν τις θελων οδον οδευειν επι τον ωρισμενον τοπον σπευση τοις εργοις αυτου. εστιν ουν η δοθεισα ημιν γνωσις του περιπατειν εν αυτη τοιαυτη· αγαπησεις τον ποιησαντα σε, φοβηθηση τον σε πλασαντα, δοξασεις τον σε λυτρωσαμενον εκ θανατου. εση απλους τη καρδια και πλουσιος τω πνευματι. ου κολληθηση μετα των πορευομενων εν οδω θανατου, μισησεις παν ο ουκ εστιν αρεστον τω θεω, μισησεις πασαν υποκρισιν· ου μαη εγκαταλιπης εντολας κυριου. ουχ υψωσεις σεαυτον, εση δε ταπεινοφρων κατα παντα. ουκ αρεις επι σεαυτον δοξαν. ου λημψη βουλην πονηραν κατα του πλησιον σου. ου δωσεις τη ψυχη σου θρασος. ου πορνευσεις, ου μοιχευσεις, ου παιδοφθορησεις. ου μη σου ο λογος του θεου εξελθη εν ακαθαρσια τινων. ου λημψη προσωπον ελεγξαι τινα επι παραπτωματι. εση πραυς, εση ησυχιος, εση τρεμων τους λογους ους ηκουσας. ου μνησικακησεις τω αδελφω σου. ου μη διψυχησης ποτερον εσται η ου. ου μη λαβης επι ματαιω το ονομα κυριου. αγαθησεις τον πλησιον σου υπηρ την ψυχην σου. ου φονευσεις τεκνον εν φθορα, ουδε παλιν γεννηθεν αποκτενεις. ου μη αρης την χειρα σου απο του υιου σου η απο της θυγατρος σου, αλλα απο νεοτητος διδαξεις φοβον θεου. ου μη γενη επιθυμων τα του πλησιον σου, ου μη γενη πλεονεκτης. ουδε κολληθηση εκ ψυχης σου μετα υψηλων, αλλα μετα ταπεινων και δικαιων αναστραφηση. τα συμβαινοντα σοι ενεργηματα ως αγαθα προσδεξη, ειδως οτι ανευ θεου ουδεν γινεται. ουκ εση διγνωμων ουδε διγλωσσος. υποταγηση κυριοις ως τυπω θεου εν αισχυνη και φοβω. ου μη επιταξης δουλω σου η παιδισκη εν πικρια, τοις επι τον αυτον θεον ελπιζουσιν, μηποτε ου μη φοβηθησονται τον επ αμφοτεροις θεον, οτι ηλθεν ου κατα προσωπον καλεσαι, αλλ εφ ους το πνευμα ητοιμασεν.

κοινωνησεις εν πασιν τω πλησιον σου, και ουκ ερεις ιδια ειναι. ει γαρ εν τω αφθαρτω κοινωνοι εστε, ποσω μαλλον εν τοις φθαρτοις. ουκ εση προγλωσσος, παγις γαρ το στομα θανατου. οσον δυνασαι υπερ της ψυχης σου αγνευσεις.

μη γινου προς μεν το λαβειν εκτεινων τας χειρας, προς δε το δουναι συσπων. αγαπησεις ως κορην του οφθαλμου σου παντα τον λαλουντα σοι τον λογον κυριου.

μνησθηση ημεραν κρισεως νυκτος και ημερας, κα εκζητησεις καθ εκαστην ημεραν τα προσωπα των αγιων, η δια λογου κοπιων και πορευομενος εις το παρακαλεσαι και μελετων εις το σωσαι ψυχην τω λογω, η δια των χειρων σου εργαση εις λυτρον αμαρτιων σου.

ου διστασεις δουναι ουδε διδους γογγυσεις, γνωση δε τις ο του μισθου καλος ανταποδοτης. φυλαξεις α παρελαβες, μητε προστιθεις μητε αφαιρων. εις τελος μισησεις τον πονηρον. κρινεις δικαιως.

ου ποιησεις σχισμα, ειρηνευσεις δε μαχομενους συναγαγων. εξομολογηση επι αμαρτιαις σου. ου προσηξεις επι προσευχην εν συνειδησει πονηρα. αυτη εστιν η οδος του φωτος.

Chapter 20

Η δε του μελανος οδος εστιν σκολια και καταρας μεστη. οδος γαρ εστιν θανατου αιωνιου μετα τιμωριας, εν η εστιν τα απολλυντα την ψυχην αυτων· ειδωλολατρεια, θρασυτης, υψος δυναμεως, υποκρισις, διπλοκαρδια, μοιχεια, φονος, αρπαγη, υπερηφανια, παραβασις, δολος, κακια, αυθαδεια, φαρμακεια, μαγεια, πλεονεξια, αφοβια θεου·

διωκται των αγαθων, μισουντες αληθειαν, αγαπωντες ψευδος, ου γινωσκοντες μισθον δικαιοσυνης, ου

116

κολλωμενοι αγαθω, ου κρισει δικαια, χηρα και ορφανω ου προσεχοντες, αγρυπνουντες ουκ εις φοβον θεου, αλλα επι το πονηρον, ων μακραν και πορρω πραυτης και υπομονη, αγαθωντες ματαια, διωκοντες ανταποδομα, ουκ ελεουντες πτωχον, ου πονουντες επι καταπονουμενω, ευχερεις εν καταλαλια, ου γινωσκοντες τον ποιησαντα αυτους, φονεις τεκνων, φθορεις πλασματος θεου, αποστρεφομενοι τον ενδεομενον, καταπονουντες τον θλιβομενον, πλουσιων παρακλητοι, πενητων ανομοι κριται, πανταμαρτητοι.

Chapter 21

Καλον ουν εστιν, μαθοντα τα δικαιωματα του κυριου οσα γεγραπται, εν τουτοις περιπατειν. ο γαρ ταυτα ποιων εν τη βασιλεια του θεου δοξασθησεται· ο εκεινα εκλεγομενος μετα των εργων αυτου συναπολειται. δια τουτο αναστασις, δια τουτο ανταποδομα.

Ερωτω τους υπερεχοντας, ει τινα μου γνωμης αγαθης λαμβανετε συμβουλιαν· εχετε μεθ εαυτων εις ους εργασεσθε το καλον· μη ελλειπητε.

εγγυς η ημερα εν η συναπολειται παντα τω πονηρω. εγγυς ο κυριος και ο μισθος αυτου.

ετι και ετι ερωτω υμας· εαυτων γινεσθε νομοθεται αγαθοι, εαυτων μενετε συμβουλοι πιστοι, αρατε εξ υμων πασαν υποκρισιν.

ο δε θεος, ο του παντος κοσμου κυριευων, δωη υμιν σοφιαν, συνεσιν, επιστημην, γνωσιν των δικαιωματων αυτου, υπομονην.

γινεσθε δε θεοδιδακτοι, εκζητουντες τι ζητει κυριος αφ υμων, και ποιειτε ινα ευρεθητε εν ημερα κρισεως.

ει δε τις εστιν αγαθου μνεια, μνημονευετε μου μελετωντες ταυτα, ινα και η επιθυμια και η αγρυπνια εις τι αγαθον χωρηση. ερωτω υμας, χαριν αιτουμενος.

εως ετι το καλον σκευος εστιν μεθ υμων, μη ελλειπητε μηδενι εαυτων, αλλα συνεχως εκζητειτε ταυτα και αναπληρουτε πασαν εντολην, εστιν γαρ αξια.

διο μαλλον εσπουδασα γραψαι αφ ων ηδυνηθην, εις το ευφραναι υμας. σωζεσθε, αγαπης τεκνα και ειρηνης. ο κυριος της δοξης και πασης χαριτος μετα του πνευματος υμων.

Other Books by
Dr. Ken Johnson

Epistle of Barnabas

Ancient Post-Flood History
Historical Documents That Point to a Biblical Creation.

This book is a Christian timeline of ancient post-Flood history based on Bible chronology, the early church fathers, and ancient Jewish and secular history. This can be used as a companion guide in the study of Creation Science.

Some questions answered: Who were the Pharaohs in the times of Joseph and Moses? When did the famine of Joseph occur? What Egyptian documents mention these? When did the Exodus take place? When did the Kings of Egypt start being called "Pharaoh" and why?

Who was the first king of a united Italy? Who was Zeus and where is he buried? Where did Shem and Ham rule and where are they buried?

How large was Nimrod's invasion force that set up the Babylonian Empire, and when did this invasion occur? What is Nimrod's name in Persian documents?

How can we use this information to witness to unbelievers?

Ancient Seder Olam
A Christian Translation of the 2000-year-old Scroll

This 2000-year-old scroll reveals the chronology from Creation through Cyrus' decree that freed the Jews in 536 BC. The *Ancient Seder Olam* uses biblical prophecy to prove its calculations of the timeline. We have used this technique to continue the timeline all the way to the reestablishment of the nation of Israel in AD 1948.

Using the Bible and rabbinical tradition, this book shows that the ancient Jews awaited King Messiah to fulfill the prophecy spoken of in Daniel, Chapter 9. The Seder answers many questions about the chronology of the books of Kings and Chronicles. It talks about the coming of Elijah, King Messiah's reign, and the battle of Gog and Magog.

This scroll and the Jasher scroll are the two main sources used in Ken's first book, *Ancient Post-Flood History*.

Epistle of Barnabas

Ancient Prophecies Revealed
500 Prophecies Listed In Order Of When They Were Fulfilled

This book details over 500 biblical prophecies in the order they were fulfilled; these include pre-flood times though the First Coming of Jesus and into the Middle Ages. The heart of this book is the 53 prophecies fulfilled between 1948 and 2008. The last 11 prophecies between 2008 and the Tribulation are also given. All these are documented and interpreted from the Ancient Church Fathers.

The Ancient Church Fathers, including disciples of the 12 apostles, were firmly premillennial, pretribulational, and very pro-Israel.

Ancient Book of Jasher
Referenced in Joshua 10:13; 2 Samuel 1:18; 2 Timothy 3:8

There are 13 ancient history books mentioned and recommended by the Bible. The Ancient Book of Jasher is the only one of the 13 that still exists. It is referenced in Joshua 10:13; 2 Samuel 1:18; and 2 Timothy 3:8. This volume contains the entire 91 chapters plus a detailed analysis of the supposed discrepancies, cross-referenced historical accounts, and detailed charts for ease of use. As with any history book, there are typographical errors in the text but with three consecutive timelines running though the histories, it is very easy to arrive at the exact dates of recorded events. It is not surprising that this ancient document confirms the Scripture and the chronology given in the Hebrew version of the Old Testament, once and for all settling the chronology differences between the Hebrew Old Testament and the Greek Septuagint. The Ancient book of Jasher is brought to you by Biblefacts Ministries, Biblefacts.org

Epistle of Barnabas

Third Corinthians
Ancient Gnostics and the End of the World

This little known, 2000-year-old Greek manuscript was used in the first two centuries to combat Gnostic cults. Whether or not it is an authentic copy of the original epistle written by the apostle Paul, it gives an incredible look into the cults that will arise in the Last Days. It contains a prophecy that the same heresies that pervaded the first century church would return before the Second Coming of the Messiah.

Ancient Paganism
The Sorcery of the Fallen Angels

Ancient Paganism explores the false religion of the ancient pre-Flood world and its spread into the Gentile nations after Noah's Flood. Quotes from the ancient church fathers, rabbis, and the Talmud detail the activities and beliefs
of both Canaanite and New Testament era sorcery. This book explores how, according to biblical prophecy, this same sorcery will return before the Second Coming of Jesus Christ to earth. These religious beliefs and practices will invade the end time church and become the basis for the religion of the Antichrist. Wicca, Druidism, Halloween, Yule, meditation, and occultic tools are discussed at length.

The Rapture
The Pretribulational Rapture of the Church Viewed From the Bible and the Ancient Church

This book presents the doctrine of the pretribulational Rapture of the church. Many prophecies are explored with Biblical passages and terms explained.

Evidence is presented that proves the first century church believed the End Times would begin with the return of Israel to her ancient homeland, followed by the Tribulation and the Second Coming. More than fifty prophecies have been fulfilled since Israel became a state.

Evidence is also given that several ancient rabbis and at least four ancient church fathers taught a pretribulational Rapture. This book also gives many of the answers to the arguments midtribulationists and posttribulationists use. It is our hope this book will be an indispensable guide for debating the doctrine of the Rapture.

Epistle of Barnabas

The Ancient Church Fathers
What the Disciples of the Apostles Taught

This book reveals who the disciples of the twelve apostles were and what they taught, from their own writings. It documents the same doctrine was faithfully transmitted to their descendants in the first few centuries and where, when, and by whom, the doctrines began to change. The ancient church fathers make it very easy to know for sure what the complete teachings of Jesus and the twelve apostles were.

You will learn, from their own writings, that the first century disciples taught on the various doctrines that divide our church today. You will learn what was discussed at the seven general councils and why. You will learn who were the cults and cult leaders that began to change doctrine and spread their heresy and how that became to be the standard teaching in the medieval church. A partial list of doctrines discussed in this book are:

Abortion	Free will	Purgatory
Animals sacrifices	Gnostic cults	Psychology
Antichrist	Homosexuality	Reincarnation
Arminianism	Idolatry	Replacement theology
Bible or tradition	Islam	Roman Catholicism
Calvinism	Israel's return	The Sabbath
Circumcision	Jewish food laws	Salvation
Deity of Jesus Christ	Mary's virginity	Schism of Nepos
Demons	Mary's assumption	Sin / Salvation
Euthanasia	Meditation	The soul
Evolution	The Nicolaitans	Spiritual gifts
False gospels	Paganism	Transubstantiation
False prophets	Predestination	Yoga
Foreknowledge	premillennialism	Women in ministry

For more information visit us at:

Biblefacts.org

Bibliography

1. Eerdmans Publishing, *Ante-Nicene Fathers*, Eerdmans Publishing, 1886.
2. Ken Johnson, *Ancient Prophecies Revealed*, Createspace, 2008
3. Ken Johnson, *Ancient Post-Flood History*, Createspace, 2010
4. Ken Johnson, *The Rapture*, Createspace, 2009
5. Ken Johnson, *Ancient Paganism*, Createspace, 2009
6. J. B. Lightfoot, *Apostolic Fathers*, Baker Books, 1891

Made in the USA
Charleston, SC
22 December 2011